AMERICA'S CUP '87

SAIL OF THE
CENTURY

Other America's Cup titles published by Stanford Maritime
Keelhauled
Unsportsmanlike Conduct and the America's Cup
by Doug Riggs

AMERICA'S CUP '87

SAIL OF THE CENTURY

Stuart Alexander
Tim Jeffery
Adrian Morgan
Chris Freer
Barry Pickthall
Jonathan Eastland

STANFORD MARITIME · LONDON

Stanford Maritime Limited
Member Company of the George Philip Group
27A Floral Street, London WC2E 9DP

First published in Great Britain 1987
© Stuart Alexander, Adrian Morgan, Tim Jeffery, Chris Freer,
Barry Pickthall, Jonathan Eastland 1987

Photos Roger Garwood, Colorific

British Library Cataloguing in Publication Data
    Sail of the century: American Cup '87.
    1. America's Cup (*1987 : Perth : Western Australia*)
    I. Alexander, Stuart
    797.1'4   GV830 1987
    ISBN 0 540 07324 5

Printed and bound by Butler & Tanner Ltd, Frome and London

Contents

Preface

To most people the America's Cup was, is, and will always be, something of a mystery. The story of the high jinks in Fremantle must have seemed an élitist waste of newsprint to those more interested in the greyhound or football results. Nevertheless, for all who remained unconverted and sceptical there were just as many for whom this sporting soap became a daily addiction. It was impossible to miss a day's account of the fortunes of the 13 Challengers and six Defenders who spent the best part of two years preparing for the Cup, and the two yachts which finally met on 31 January to decide the outcome of the oldest continual sporting contest between two nations.

This book is not a blow-by-blow account of the races – that would be tedious – but rather an attempt by a handful of Cup watchers to capture, in their own words, what it was like to be in Fremantle when Australia first defended the Cup, and some of the background to the Sail of the Century.

Introduction

The America's Cup has always been a game played by the rich for high stakes. Over the last 136 years gentlemen have come to blows over it, fortunes have been lost through it and diplomatic relations have been strained because of it. Underneath all the hype and skulduggery, however, the America's Cup is a yacht race and those who have tried to hijack it for their own purposes have never quite managed to detract from that reality: a supreme test of sailing skill between finely tuned yachts with tall sails that shine like raised swords in the sun.

In Perth throughout the long build up to the America's Cup Summer it was at times hard to believe that behind all the hype there was a yacht race going on at all. Only slowly did the true heroines and heroes emerge – the yachts and the crews that sailed them. To those who have never been interested in yachting at any level the spectacle came as a pleasant surprise. While sports editors scratched their heads and tried to come to grips with a sport hitherto regarded as obscure, the specialist yachting press poured forth. And yet very few of those who read about the 1987 series had any chance of seeing at first hand what was going on.

Above all America's Cup racing is a beautiful, if at times nauseous, sport to watch. The unknowing and unsuspecting journalists and the tourists who were lured to Fremantle, learnt quickly to take their seasickness tablets. Those with no stomach for the trip soon forsook the decks of the Press and spectator boats for the safety and stability of the nearest bar with a television, and a 'tinnie' near at hand. They may have seen it, but only those who watched the racing caught the spirit of the Cup. For them the America's Cup became an obsession.

For the true believer, the America's Cup aficionado, it was an addiction stronger than any narcotic. Unlike other forms of yacht racing where the results are often confused by time allowances and handicaps; where the first across the line is very seldom the winner, the America's Cup is a test of nerve and aggression between two boats, two skippers and ultimately two countries – head to head, bow to bow; the closest thing to unarmed combat outside a boxing ring.

America rules the waves

Beautiful to watch, exclusive, newsworthy at times, the outcome of the America's Cup had until 1983 been entirely predictable. For well over a century the America's Cup, named not after the country but after the schooner *America* which first won it in 1851, belonged almost as if by right to the Americans in general and to the exclusive New York Yacht Club in particular. In 24 matches few challenging yachts had come close to winning it. It was never dull, but it was seldom close fought. It was usually a question not of whether the Americans would win but by how much.

That all changed on 26 September 1983. The next day Newport, Rhode Island, a small town in New England with a sign in the main street saying 'Home of the America's Cup', woke up with a massive hangover and, as one writer put it 'the sickening feeling that it had been mugged'. A winged-keel yacht from Western Australia had waltzed off with their prized possession. For some inexplicable reason a sport which has seldom hit the headlines became front page news. It was suddenly naïve to think of it just as a yacht race. Civic pride bedamn'd; national pride was now at stake. The Americans realised that the trophy they had held for so long was off on a long journey.

An estimated $200 million was spent by those taking part – a nautical arms race; an obscene figure. America alone built 12 yachts to bring it back home. If it was bad enough spending money on ballistic missiles it was doubly so on a yacht race. The money invested in aluminium and lead, sailcloth and stainless steel would have fed Ethiopia for a year.

This seems to miss the point. The capital city and an economy of a state the size of Western Europe depended on it for a few months; thousands of new jobs were created by it. The America's Cup was Western Australia's answer to the Gold Rush.

Over $AUS2 billion were invested to stage it and retain it; and the best sportswriters in the world went to Fremantle to watch them do it. Why was this so?

To answer that question you must go back to 1851 when that black schooner *America* visited Britain's shores. She was designed expressly for the purpose of winning money through wagers on yacht races. She proved so fast in informal races that no-one was prepared to meet her. No-one was prepared to lose. Finally the Royal Yacht Squadron put up a trophy, valued in those days at 100 guineas – an ornate, some think rather ugly, ewer made by Garrards, the crown jewellers, in 1848 containing 134oz of fine Sterling Silver with an intrinsic value of just $US800. Under the concerned gaze of Queen Victoria she defeated the country's crack racing fleet in a 60-mile course round the Isle of Wight. The '100 Guinea Cup' became the schooner '*America*'s Cup'.

Britain's humiliation in the year of the Great Exhibition shook the yachting establishment out of the complacency of Empire. In sciences Britannia ruled the waves but she evidently had a lot to learn about yacht design. The victory of the 170-ton Yankee schooner rankled.

Like Goliath sent to teach young David a lesson, Britain sent yachts across the Atlantic to recover the Cup. They all returned humbled and humiliated. The two Canadian Challenges fared little better. Even against a superior yacht the Americans found some way to retain their unbeaten record – usually by better sailing, sometimes by changing the rules at crucial moments and even, some say, by downright ungentlemanly behaviour. But it would be wrong to think that yachting in those early days was anything other than a cut-throat business. Too much pride was at stake. Too much money spent.

In 1934 when Tom Sopwith's *Endeavour* came close to lifting the Cup off its pedestal the New York Yacht Club came under intense criticism. 'Britannia Rules the Waves but America Waives the Rules' went the famous, and oft-quoted headline.

Britain came no closer to winning it than in that year. Her post-war record was frankly embarrassing. The will to win was not lacking, it was just that Britain no longer seemed able to afford it. Even in 1958 when the rules were changed to outlaw the enormous and extravagant 120-footers in favour of the much smaller 12 Metre Class it was an expensive business.

In 1964, for example, anticipating a strong British assault,

America campaigned five yachts in the Defender trials, two of them brand new. Enormous sums were spent preparing for the forthcoming contest. In the ensuing fiasco the British entry proved so slow that any ten-year old yacht could have beaten her comfortably. It was none too tactfully suggested that Britain should step aside and let someone else have a crack.

That someone was a dynamic Australian tycoon called Sir Frank Packer who had challenged earlier in 1962. He had little better luck again in 1970 but at least gave the Americans a run for their money. But it was to be 21 years before the Australians began to get the measure of the Americans. In 1983, after three previous attempts, another Australian tycoon, Alan Bond, born in Ealing, West London, took a gamble and financed the building of a yacht so radical and so fast that it took the Americans by surprise.

Victory of the New New World
Complacent they were not, but years of victory, often in slower but better-sailed boats had blunted their ability to produce breakthrough designs. By the time they realised what they were up against in *Australia II* it was almost too late.

The rest of the story is well documented. First they tried to outlaw *Australia II* as a rule-cheater but failed. Then they discussed pulling out of the race at the eleventh hour, but that was unthinkable. Finally they decided to trust in the skills of their best helmsman, Dennis Conner. If he failed on the tricky waters of Newport Sound they would replace the Cup with his head. The gamble very nearly paid off. In a cliffhanging best-of-seven race series the Australian yacht was triumphant. Conner kept his head but lost the Cup. The symbolic victory of the New New World over the Old New World was complete.

The Old New World was not amused. Almost immediately plans were made to recapture the Cup, funds were pledged, computer time booked. It was lost. It would return. It wasn't war this time; it was far more important. It was a matter of honour. And that probably explains why the land of the Pilgrim Fathers spent so much in an attempt to recapture their lost heritage – a Cup they consider to have been bushwacked by a bunch of sailors from Down Under with a tradition even shorter than theirs. It did not, however, explain the interest shown by the other five countries, Britain, France, New Zealand, Canada and Italy.

For this, one has to look not at the intrinsic or otherwise value of the America's Cup itself but of the benefits that accrue to any nation whose sailors, sailmakers and yacht designers are skilful enough to win it. Before the outcome last February Western Australia reckoned that the Cup was worth from $600 million to $1.1 billion to the economy. A state that would stretch from Norway to Malta north to south and Western Ireland to the Berlin Wall from west to east saw its population increase by 500,000 at times during the America's Cup Summer.

Only now can the victors and the vanquished assess whether it has all been worth the trouble. Yacht race it may well have been, but to the people of whichever town or city the circus will now descend on it means wealth and jobs and the focus of world-wide media attention. To the winner go the spoils – the least of which is an ornate Victorian ewer.

Whether the enormous expenditure was justified depends on your opinion of yacht racing. To send the British yacht *White Crusader* to Perth cost about £5 million. Was it worth it? for that you'll have to ask the multinationals like Guinness, who pledged over £1 million to the British campaign, or the big banks who backed the Kiwis, or Fiat who kept an Italian syndicate in Perth long after their chances seemed hopeless or Coca Cola and Amway who invested so heavily in the American syndicates or the giant photographic firm Kis who named their yacht *French Kiss*. Probably only one organisation made a profit and that was Mark McCormack's mighty IMG marketing empire. The America's Cup is big business. Every dollar earning angle was explored.

On the Australian side things were much the same. Swan Brewery, Hong Kong and Shanghai Bank, Woolworths, Qantas, Data General, Citizen Watches, Rank Xerox, Schweppes, Seiko, Olivetti, Mitsubishi, Australian Airlines, Mobil, Yamaha, Digital Computer, Nike, Ansett, Panasonic – even the City of Sydney, whose yacht was called *Steak 'n' Kidney* – hitched their stars on the outcome of a yacht race that became the focus of world-wide media interest.

This nautical version of Star Wars, played out within the mega memories of the world's most powerful computers, will probably never again be repeated on the same scale. The stakes are too high, the penalties for failure too steep. Grumman, British Aerospace and the French Aerospatiale donated computer time to designers in the search for a yacht even more radical than the winged-keel *Australia II*. A plateau has now been reached. Further gains will cost even more dearly.

The days when model yachts not warships provided the biggest tank-testing facilities in the world with the major source of their income are probably over. This time around every yacht had a secret keel. In 1983 the Australians built a plywood and sailcloth shield round their yacht to hide it from prying eyes. In Perth barbed wire fences, security guards, underwater steel doors and fierce dogs were *de rigueur*. Spy planes and mini submarines all played their part in the arms race. It seems faintly ridiculous now.

As usual the outcome rested eventually on the crews. Fortunes ultimately rested on the strong shoulders of those who hauled sails and ground winches. By 31 January the 13 challenging yachts and six defending yachts had been whittled down to just two. Defeated Challengers packed up and left for home de-dollared and dispirited, the seas off Fremantle were at last clear for a best-of-seven match series between the two chosen yachts.

For the crews of those two yachts it was 'just a yacht race' – albeit the hardest, most physically demanding and psychologically crippling yacht race ever devised.

CHAPTER ONE

The Best Kept Secret

Tim Jeffery

Three o'clock in the morning is no time to discover a foreign city, but that's when visitors from Europe get their first taste of Perth, its tall office buildings visible far off from inbound flights, lights reflecting in the black waters of the Swan River.

American broadcaster Walter Kronkite described Perth as 'the best kept secret in the World'. Until John Bertrand and the crew of *Australia II* crossed the finishing line of the seventh race of the 1983 America's Cup 41 seconds ahead of Dennis Conner's *Liberty*, Perth remained a secret. Little had happened to put it on the world stage.

Then, quite suddenly, everyone wanted to know. *Australia II*'s victory put Western Australia's capital on the map. Western countries with an interest in the America's Cup found Perth on the other side of the world, at the end of the airlines' longest routes; British Airways, Qantas and Singapore Airlines were among the few that went there at all. Only when the cabins had been sprayed with insecticide were the passengers allowed to disgorge into the hot night air of Western Australia. Perth's air services are a telling reminder of her remoteness.

Travellers on British Airways are a lucky minority; they can stay on their plane throughout the 24-hour journey. There are no transfers to make, no planes to switch or connections to make. Americans have a rougher deal. They route through Los Angeles and thence to Sydney to catch an internal flight to Western Australia.

Arthur Wullschleger, shore boss of the New York Yacht Club's *America II* Syndicate in nearby Fremantle, is a man with a nice line in dry humour. He used to tell visitors to his headquarters that directly below them lay the north-eastern seaboard of the United States. If they burrowed through the earth's axis they would emerge about 100 miles from Newport, Rhode Island, home of the Cup for so many years. It was an exaggeration; but it made the point.

Remote, relatively inaccessible, nevertheless even in the early hours Perth has an air of excitement.

Boom Town

On the road from the airport visitors can hardly fail to notice the new Burswood Island Resort. Before the 1983 America's Cup, the site was a rubbish dump. Now from the final resting place for Perth's refuse, the bright lights of one of the world's largest gaming resorts, and the largest in the southern Hemisphere, glow late into the night. This $300 million playground is so large that only the new parliament development in Canberra beats it in the Australian construction league table. As for tables, the casino house has 137 of them, while the sports, entertainment and conference facilities can cope with 17,000 visitors.

The idea of turning the city rubbish dump into a five-star complex belonged to the appropriately named Dallas Dempster. His development typifies the bullish belief of Western Australians in their state. Before *Australia II* made sporting history, the local WA car number plates carried the slogan 'The State of Excitement'; afterwards they read 'Home of the America's Cup'.

Australia II's win set in motion a rush of development in what was already a very active city. Burswood Island was just one example. Built in less than two years it made a profit in its first year with 8500 visitors per day. But in the heart of downtown Perth, signs of prosperity and growth were equally evident. Along Perth's vital artery, the windy St George's Terrace, tower blocks reach into the deep blue sky, the concrete and steel structures in curious contrast to the crenellated colonial-style buildings from Perth's fledgling years. Tucked among the lush trees and shrubs near Barrack Street is Government House, the epitome of 19th-century, baronial-style architecture. It would not look amiss in Merseyside's merchant trader residential belt of Chester and the Wirral.

Unlike Liverpool, Perth is the tiny capital city of an enormous state in a huge country. With just under a million inhabitants it is smaller than many provincial cities in Europe and the

States, yet it is the most important centre in a state large enough to swallow most of Europe. Western Australia could take Texas, New Zealand and Japan for good measure, and still have room to spare.

Just what makes Western Australia the 'State of Excitement' goes beyond post-colonial bullishness. Perth may be perched 2500 miles away from the legislative and commercial centres of Canberra and Sydney, but it is Western Australia's trading post for her vast natural resources; massive iron ore deposits, nickel ores, bauxite, natural gas and petroleum, gold, mineral sands, coal, copper, zinc, uranium and diamonds. Clearly Western Australia was at the head of the queue when the world's mineral riches were handed out. To some extent these resources have accounted for the state's boom-bust economic cycle though the economic base is much wider these days and less sensitive to cyclical effects. It was such natural resources which laid the foundations for Western Australia's present position.

The state was first visited at least 20,000 years ago by inhabitants of southern Asia, the first Aborigines, but her known history is relatively short. Early in the 1600s the Dutch were the first European visitors, sailing up and down, and frequently onto, the shore of Western Australia. Like the wrecking of their ships, the Dutch visits ashore were not intentional. Strong westerly winds blew vessels on the Holland–East Indies trade route off-course. In 1644, Dutch explorer Abel Tasman was dispatched by the Dutch East India Company to the northwest coast of Australia. Although he found the land arid and the nomadic Aboriginal inhabitants unwelcoming, Tasman nevertheless called the land New Holland.

The British came around 1800, but were generally unenthusiastic, unlike Captain Cook who had discovered the east coast with *Endeavour* in 1770 and claimed it for the Crown, calling it New South Wales. By the 1820s the British were back on the west coast, charting its features. Captain Stirling of HMS *Success* found the Swan River. Thinking it a much better place for a settlement, he sent word to London. Finally, in 1828, a Captain Fremantle was dispatched in HMS *Challenger* to claim the western third of Australia for the British Crown. So while in 1986/87 Western Australia played host to the biggest yachting, indeed sporting event ever, the history of the host state is only 23 years longer than that of the America's Cup itself.

The early settlers did not prosper until gold was found in the

1880s with even bigger strikes at Kalgoorlie and Coolgardie in 1892 and 1893. The population increased seven times in just 20 years, though it was not until the 1960s that investment in other mineral resources took place on a large scale. In the meantime the rural economy was pre-eminent; the vast tracts of sparsely populated land being used for sheep, wheat and cattle.

Much produce is still exported. Western Australian farmers are world leaders in dry farming techniques – they need to be with a climate which is Mediterranean on the coast and desert inland – while there is a steady export of live sheep to the Muslim markets of the Middle East. America's Cup crews, well known for their base humour, christened the ships which carry the sheep 'Kiwi Love Boats' and lorries which take them to the docks 'Kiwi Tour Buses'. The ships themselves resemble multi-storey car parks.

There are also surprising exports. Lupins, high in polyunsaturated oils and proteins, are a big earner on the Japanese market.

Fishing
But it is fish which brings in Fremantle's income, Western Australia's original settlement; a boom town in the era of immigration, gold exploitation and the arrival of the railway. Before the Cup, the city which lies at the entrance to the Swan River, some 12 miles downstream from Perth, was showing signs of decay, of past glories fast fading. Like parts of Perth which had not been redeveloped, Fremantle was colonial; timber buildings, open verandahs, corrugated iron roofs and grand facades with filligree ironwork and stuccoed facings. Sadly the more elegant buildings had degenerated, disfigured by advertising hoardings and garish shop fronts of neon and Perspex. The Cup, at least, brought smartness to Fremantle and with the Australian bi-centenery in 1988 massive amounts of central government funds are now swelling the city and state coffers. Easy elegance has returned with the Cup.

Before the Cup circus descended on this relic of colonial times the large Fishing Boat and Success harbours were home to the inelegant crayfish and rock lobster boats which plied their six-months-a-year trade. The strong Italian community, above all, enjoyed lucrative trade links with the USA and Japan.

Shellfish and other varieties are not the only harvests to be reaped from the plentiful seas. Western Australia has had a strong tradition in pearl fishing centred on Broome in the north-west. Indeed some of the old Broome sailing luggers were on charter agents' lists for hire during the Cup months.

The 23,000 inhabitants of Fremantle had mixed feelings about the America's Cup invasion. Some threw their lot quickly and unashamedly in with it, selling bottled Indian Ocean water, opening bars, printing T-shirts in expectation of the influx of visiting yachtsmen and their entourages. Others were less welcoming, expressing themselves in graffiti with explicit suggestions about where the Cup should be put.

The work-day fishing boats have had to share the hugely expanded harbour with ritzy motor and sailing yachts more used to the flesh pots of Palma, Antibes and Porto Cervo, or English Harbour Antigua and Pier 69 in Fort Lauderdale. One of these was Alan Bond's new *Southern Cross III*, styled by Jon Bannenburg in Chelsea, but built by Sterling Shipyard in Japan. The furore surrounding Bond's decision not to build in Australia was one of the seamier episodes the ebullient tycoon faced on inheriting the title 'The Man Who Won the Cup'.

First Fremantle's dock workers threatened to black the yacht. Presumably they thought they could afford to cold shoulder the home-town hero and his modest 180-footer when the *Sea Goddess* and *Achille Lauro* cruised into town.

Bond also incurred the wrath of the construction workers, many of whom, adopting the traditions of the Old Country, had become heavily unionised. They clashed over the building of his Observation City, a $100 million resort whose 337 bedrooms overlook Gage Roads, scene of the Cup races. Bond himself booked the Penthouse floor of the development, a three-bedroomed suite called the *Australia II* Suite, decorated subtly in the Australian national colours of green and gold, with everything you would expect in a tycoon's eyrie; grand piano, lounge, bar, separate butler's entrance and a spectacular view out over the Indian Ocean and the Cup course itself.

But before the hotel could be completed the self-made millionaire had to cope with strikes, bomb threats against his 12 Metres and demands from the workers for a 'Cup Allowance' who played their trump card cynically in the negotiations over meeting the Cup deadline. Another Bond building, a crew headquarters just opposite Marine Terrace, opposite the dock, never got off the ground at all.

Other Fremantle inhabitants welcomed the money-laden Cup

juggernaut with open arms. Don Wierenga, for example, found himself sitting on the prime real estate in town. Whereas before his Fremantle Boat Lifters site had docked and serviced the crayfish boats, by early 1984 high-powered Americans were knocking on his door asking if they could berth their 12 Metres and luxury syndicate yachts. He was soon in the tempting position of being able to play off the two most-fancied and best-financed American groups, each trying to outbid the other. Finally William Packer, Vice Chairman of the New York Yacht Club's *America II* group clinched the deal with a $10,000 personal cheque as down payment. One of several Texas oilmen, power brokers behind *America II*, Packer flew Wierenga to New York to clinch the deal and to show the down-to-earth Fremantle fisherman a bit of top-drawer hospitality at the New York Yacht Club's clubhouse on West 44th Street.

Dennis Conner from the rival San Diego-based Sail America group tried to persuade Wierenga to accept a better deal, 'I don't care what they've offered you', he told the astonished Wierenga. 'We'll double it.' But the fisherman stuck to his original deal and on the Fremantle Boat Lifters site he built what is probably the best 12 Metre facility in the world; so good that Kevin Parry's Taskforce '87 group also bought space for his *Kookaburra* campaign.

Few people, however, really appreciated the transformation of the America's Cup from a quasi-Corinthian event in 1983 to a fully professional regatta, now poised to become an open circuit just like golf or tennis. In Newport, few syndicates had more than one new Twelve, one tender, a few cramped dock offices and a single hoist with which to lift the boat out of the water after racing.

The *America II* compound had two hoists, which could be caged off from prying eyes; a village of offices, stores and workshops made from air-conditioned shipping containers. There was a shed so big that a 12 Metre could be wheeled straight in, cradled in a monster mobile hoist and enough floor space to work on the yacht's sails. Alongside the compound there was sufficient dock space to berth three 150ft luxury yachts; one belonging to Packer himself and another *Enterprise IV*, owned by Rich de Vos and his direct-sell company, Amway, the major commercial sponsor of the New York Yacht Club effort. Just to reinforce the point that mounting an America's Cup campaign on the other side of the world was a complicated venture almost beyond comprehension, the *America II* compound had its own electricity generation plant. All the machine tools and computing facility ran on American-cycle electricity. Aussie juice was not acceptable.

Another of the Fremantle entrepreneurs, Mick Lombardo, built a new restaurant complex right on the harbour's edge. Its spaceship styling now contains all manner of dining facilities, ranging from take-away fish and chip stalls to a rather elegant *à la carte* restaurant for even the most cosmopolitan of international visitors. The Lombardo's complex was the latest chapter in a family history which began with Vincenzo Lombardo, a Sicilian who jumped ship in 1922 as a non-English-speaking 12-year-old with only fishing skills to his name.

Alan Bond, another migrant who made his fortune in Western Australia, also arrived by ship. Like Vincenzo Lombardo, Bond was something of a child prodigy, showing a flair for making money at an early age. At school, he bought his own stock of newspapers to sell to other boys after the newspaper shop shut, so that they could do extended newspaper rounds. His father allowed him to leave school at 15 provided that the young Bond learnt a skill. He took up signwriting and visitors making their way to Fremantle from Perth along the Stirling Highway pass a huge red dingo painted on a flour mill which faces out over the ocean. It was the sort of job Bond would do and others wouldn't; tough, dangerous and financially rewarding.

At 18 he married Eileen, daughter of a Fremantle businessman and politician. The day after their wedding Bond bought a plot of land, divided it, and sold the sub plots. By the age of 22 he was a dollar millionaire and Perth's first high-rise blocks began to soar into the sky. Ten years later he was Western Australia's most active property developer, an interested yachtsman and owner of the crack ocean racer, *Apollo*. In 1974 he financed his first of four America's Cup bids, spending some $16 million of his own money in all. This was a triflingly small sum. The Cup allowed him to raise money at home and gain *entrées* in the USA. His patriotic Cup bids kept the creditors from his door during tough times in the 1970s, while he delved into gas exploration and other business fields. By the time Bond's gamble with *Australia II* paid off in 1983, he was a businessman playing on a world stage. Brewing, real estate, diamonds, gold, oil, gas, media are now all part of the Bond Corporation.

Bond is just getting into his stride. Observers say a $20 million profit in 1985 increased 20-fold by the time Bond's final Cup campaign was concluded. From being owner of a company ranked in the 50s in Australia he has shot to a place in the top ten. According to Warren Jones, a senior executive of a private holding company who also orchestrates the Bond's Cup campaigns, Australia is now too small for The Man.

London has already felt the slipstream of Bond's high-risk, whirlwind business deals. In 1986 he bought and sold the rump of the British film industry, EMI, for £25 million profit; all in a fortnight. Apart from making sure the world knows about his Swan and Castlemaine beers, Bond has turned the ailing British Airship Industries into a company now poised to secure either a huge US Coastguard 'eye in the sky' contract or a massive aerial advertising platform, or both.

Millionaires

Bond is not the only tall poppy to have blossomed in Perth. His arch America's Cup defence rival, Kevin Parry, also used a yachting event as a launch-pad for his business empire. So committed is he to following the path carved out by Bond, that Parry signed up key personnel for the 1990 America's Cup four months before the 1987 series had run its final course.

Like Bond, Parry started small, taking on his father's cheap furniture business. An ex-soccer player, and a good one at that, Parry invested heavily in soccer and snooker before signing up Iain Murray to lead the $25 million Taskforce '87 effort. Parry's empire, already far outgrown from its furniture base, is now expanding faster than ever, taking in television, satellite launches, mineral exploration in Indonesia and hi-tech marine research. Having bought a large parcel of coastal land at Mandurah, 80 miles south of Fremantle, Parry is not only developing housing but has plans to install a test tank and full research facility to serve the increasingly industrialised Far East.

Other examples of Western Australian entrepreneurial enterprise abound. Robert Holmes à Court made his big break by buying Australia's cheapest quoted business, the Broken Hill Company. His Bell Group is now big in Australia, London and the USA. And there's Dennis Horgan whose Barrack House merchant bank started up Australia's most expensive and prestigious winery down south on the Margaret River. Its award-winning Chardonnay and the fact that Horgan, a patron of the arts, flew all 166 members of the London Philharmonic Orchestra out to his Leeuwin estate for a one-off concert, helped put the wine on the vineous map.

Among Barrack House's interesting developments has been the financing of a new type of rotary internal combustion engine offering significant gains in fuel efficiency and emission control. The first engines have been built in the States and this long-shot investment has brought in foreign currency earnings from Japan as well.

If any doubts about the vitality of Western Australia's entre-preneurs remain, then consider the fact that Perth has more millionaires per capita than any other city in the world. There are a lot of large fish swimming in this particular small pool. They have the cars – Rolls Royces go entirely unremarked – and homes to prove it.

Few cities could offer a better venue from which to make a base. The climate is moderate in winter and very hot in summer. People tend to dress informally, or smart casual as the Americans would say, though some of the older members of the community would not dream of wearing shorts without long socks. The Swan River itself is something outside of the experience of most of us – a river clean enough to swim in running through a capital city. You can hire sailboards and dinghies within yards of the downtown business district. Further downstream towards Fremantle are beaches, parks, yacht clubs and expensive resi-dential areas like Millionaires' Row in Dalkeith where the likes of Bond and Parry house themselves and their art collections.

To the visitor everything is very American. You could imagine yourself in Florida. The roads are wide, the traffic moves at a leisurely pace. The road signs are definitely American. The shops are grouped in neighbourhood 'malls' while lawns are well tended and watered. It's also a place where the beer has two prices; one for normal beer off the shelves, and a chilled price for those stored in the cool cabinets.

Nevertheless, despite Perth's undoubted attractions, right up until the Cup Finals there were few signs of the promised tourism bonanza. It's been called the 'L.A. Syndrome'. Fear of overcrowding kept the crowds away until the last moment. On 31 January, the day for the first race of the Finals, 25 flights came into Perth from Sydney, Melbourne, Brisbane and Adelaide.

The state did as much as it could to attract people to their 'State of Excitement'. Everything possible was marshalled to make sure that Perth and Fremantle cashed in on their unexpected windfall and established tourism as an industry for the future. The University of Western Australia's Centre for Applied Business Research originally estimated that the five months of Trials and Finals would bring in no fewer than half a million visitors.

Dame Edna Everidge appeared in outlandish green and gold, black swan spectacles and was filmed feeding caviar to the Fremantle seagulls as part of massive televised promotion. The bus services crossing the emptiness of the Nullarbar desert increased to five a day to bring people in from the east coast. And not all came to watch the yachting. The Western Australians bathed in a summer of sport which included no fewer than 29 sporting and cultural international events, including a West Indies–Australia–England–Pakistan cricket competition and a heavyweight boxing bout.

There was also a more serious side to it, if sport at this level could be called anything less than serious. A conference for Pacific nations, attended by 250 leaders in finance, trade, investment and government was staged in Perth in an attempt to prove that the future lay in Western Australia. Over 2000 miles from Sydney and Melbourne, Perth is no longer a well-kept secret. The place has taken a centre-stage role in Pacific basin affairs, an area analysts predict will be the fulcrum of world development in the next century.

The America's Cup has simply accelerated that rush towards the year 2000.

CHAPTER TWO

The Twelve Metre Yacht

Adrian Morgan

The story of the 12 Metre Class has become inextricably linked with that of the America's Cup, but this was by no means always the case. Born in 1906 as a result of a simple rule that aimed to produce inexpensive racing – by the standards of the day – between boats of similar size, the 12 Metre is now probably the most extravagant example of the designer's art – a yacht become so inbred and so specialised that it is useless for anything but the perennial struggles for the most coveted trophy in yacht racing.

The Class has come a long way from the early gaff-rigged Twelves of the 1900s to the extraordinary winged-keel *Australia II* and her descendants. The yacht has come to represent the greatest aspirations as well as the worst fears of those who have sought to keep the sport within the bounds of common sense and Corinthian ideals – the innocent vehicle for power struggles not only between rival designers but between countries.

Despite having been overtaken by a destiny, the 12 Metre's development has been accelerated by her association with the contest; the yachts themselves remain surprisingly majestic, stunningly beautiful with a personality and serenity that transcend the murky, acrimonious battles fought between those who have been privileged to own these remarkable throw-backs to an era when yacht racing was still the sport of gentlemen.

Construction and sailing techniques have evolved enormously over the last 80 years. From *Vim*, the pre-war Twelve that became the bench-mark for all post-war yachts, through *Intrepid*, Sparkman and Stephens' breakthrough, to the glass-fibre yachts built by the New Zealanders.

Yachts were originally created by eye, the purely personal approach enshrined in the phrase 'if it looks right, it probably is'. Now they are the result of tank-testing and calculation and not rule-of-thumb. Although a blind faith in the results of tank-testing, often at too small a scale to be of value in the real thing, has lead to some very strange and spectacularly unsuccessful yachts, like the American *Mariner*, it is now accepted that only a massive investment in computer time can produce the minute increases in performance that can lead to victory on the race course.

Nevertheless the child-like inspiration of designers like William Fife who would whittle hull shapes and leave them lying around his office until slowly day by day the right shape would emerge, and Ben Lexcen whose daydreaming lead to *Australia II* and her remarkable keel, still play their part. It is doubly ironic that a rule designed to prevent wild flights of fancy should in fact have forced designers to think so laterally. The rule makers of 1906 could hardly have imagined how far their initial ideas should have become distorted and modified by the inventive brains of a succession of brilliant naval architects, and in particular Olin Stephens, the man responsible for five of the seven post-war America's Cup winners.

Left to its own devices the 12 Metre yacht would probably have perished in the face of economic pressures. The America's Cup has given the Class unwelcome exposure at times but has also saved this relic of a bygone age against all odds and stimulated interest in yacht design in a way that those early rule makers could never have imagined in their wildest dreams. Now, with the impetus of the Cup, the Class is flourishing as never before.

When the 12 Metre Class first saw the light of day in the early years of the century they were among the smallest Classes of racing yacht – ladies' yachts. An owner might build a 12 Metre to provide his sons or daughters with their first taste of yachting.

A present day 12 Metre bears only a passing resemblance to its forbears, but little or none to the mighty 120-footers that used to race for the America's Cup. War and a changing economic climate put paid to them just as weather changes killed off the dinosaurs in prehistoric times.

The Rule

Since 1958, the first match following the war, the America's Cup has been sailed in 12 Metres. The International 12 Metre Class Rule is one of the oldest and strictest ever devised. As with any rule it was framed as an attempt to produce a standard type of yacht that would remain relatively unchanged and thus give good sport between competitors.

The Rule runs to over 20 pages of finely worded text. The first thing to grasp is that a 12 Metre yacht is not about 36 ft long. In fact it is built to a bewildering formula the product of which must be equal to, or less than 12 m or 39.37 ft. Most 12 Metre yachts are about 65 ft long with a mast height of about 80 ft and weigh about 25 tons. This is the vital formula:

$$12\,m = \frac{L + 2d - F + \sqrt{SA}}{2.37}$$

L = The length of the hull measured approximately 180 mm above the waterline. Corrections for girth are applied to this measurement.

d = The length of an imaginary line stretched from the edge of the deck to a point about halfway down the keel subtracted from the distance around the hull from the edge of the deck to a point about halfway down the keel.

SA = Sail area, including mainsail and the area of the triangle bounded by the mast, forestay and deck.

F = Freeboard, or height of hull above the waterline.

2.37 = The mathematical constant.

By juggling the various parameters, sail area, length and freeboard a designer will try to produce a hull which is faster than his competitor. He may decide that 70 ft, rather than, say, 63 ft, is the ideal length for his 12 Metre, but he then must pay a penalty by cutting the sail area.

On the other hand he may decide that a larger sail area, giving more power, is better than length, but whatever values he chooses the product of the formula must not exceed that magical figure of 12 m, or 39.37 ft.

Designers have tried many ways of finding a way to beat the Rule, some successful, some spectacularly unsuccessful. Over the years, as a result of many tests both on the water and in special model test tanks, designers have discovered that a hull length of about 65–70 ft is ideal and increasingly have turned their attention to other factors like keel shape and more efficient sail design.

In 1983 the Australian designer Ben Lexcen produced the famous 'winged keel' which was instrumental in giving his yacht *Australia II* victory over the American yacht *Liberty* – a much more conventional design.

The Crew

There is nothing on a 12 Metre yacht's deck that is either superfluous, overweight or inefficient. The deck layout is totally functional from bow to stern with a place for everything and everything in its place. There are no frills or fancies. The deck is brutal and austere, a platform on which the crew are expected to work until they drop or the race is won, whichever happens sooner.

Safety and comfort take a back seat on a 12 Metre. There are no guardrails to stop the crew falling over the side. The most cruelly exposed crew member of all, the bowman, works the pointed end at the constant mercy of breaking seas, using his knees to grip the forestay and both hands for the ship, yet woe betide him if he falls off.

Just about the only concession to safety is the non-slip deck paint. In heavy seas, when the decks are awash, even this is scarcely adequate.

The powerhouse of a 12 Metre is the central cockpit, dominated by two huge 'coffee grinder' winches used to control the headsail, the yacht's 'main engine'. The grinding cranks are placed to give the two grinders maximum leverage. In a close upwind tacking duel they may be called upon to work continuously as the helmsman attacks his opponent time after time, trying to force an error.

Behind the grinders on either side stand the two trimmers, responsible for deciding exactly how much tension the sail requires to form a perfect aerofoil to the wind. Grinders respond to the trimmers' calls.

The nerve centre of a 12 Metre lies at the stern where skipper, navigator and helmsman make and carry out the vital decisions about where to steer, when to tack and how best to attack. The navigator monitors the powerful computers which show precisely where the yacht is in relation to the opposition and how far to the next mark. Instruments read out wind speed and direction, boatspeed and efficiency for the helmsman/tactician. The dials confirm whether he is steering the boat to her best speed.

Hull and Keel Design

A 12 Metre yacht, like any boat, can be regarded simply as a hole in the water. Its speed depends on how well the water can tolerate that boat-shaped hole as it passes through. It is the designer's task to find out what the water will or will not tolerate.

The ingenious 12 Metre Class Rule permits designers a degree of freedom to which they have never been slow to respond. The problem is simple to state but hard to solve. How do you design a hull shape which is both fast and within the Rule? The Rule penalises speed producing factors. Of the many parameters which affect speed, therefore, which should be incorporated and which ignored?

In their search for answers designers have progressed from rule-of-thumb and eye to the most sophisticated tank and computer aided design facilities to find a shape which is both fast and legal.

Some, like Philippe Briand, designer of the brilliant *French Kiss*, have paid scant attention to the Rule and concentrated on a fast boat, accepting the penalties the rule imposes on fast boats and trusting that their creation is faster than the rule thinks it is. Others have concentrated on minimising the effects of the Rule and finding loopholes, like Ian Howlett's *White Crusader*.

The basic parameters of the Rule are length of hull and sail area. The problem facing the designer is whether to increase sail area at the expense of length or vice versa.

Up until 1983 most designers thought that development had reached a peak. *Australia II* changed all that. Her arrival on the Newport scene condemned every 12 Metre ever built to obscurity. Not only was she light and long, but stiff and stable. While other designers concentrated on hull shape, *Australia II*'s delightfully eccentric self-taught designer Ben Lexcen turned his fertile mind equally to keel shape. The one feature that everyone had ignored made her a winner and put her straight into the history books.

Lexcen built a light boat and put the ballast that gives any boat stability where it was most effective, right low down at the bottom of the keel in the form of lead wings.

The keel of a yacht works in water in the same way as the sails do in air, creating lift but also providing stability. Lexcen's keel was unique in that it provided more lift and more stability for the same weight than a conventional keel. Lexcen, in effect, took an old-style keel, turned it upside down and stuck it on the bottom of a lightweight hull.

The keel had other advantages. It made her more manoeuvrable and cut out some of the turbulence that made a conventional keel inefficient in comparison. But more important, perhaps, the fear of the keel caused the Americans to panic and that, ultimately, was why they lost the Cup.

No sooner was Ben Lexcen's revolutionary winged keel unveiled on 26 September, the historic day in 1983 when *Australia II* returned triumphant from her last race victory over the American yacht *Liberty*, than designers all over the world were copying, modifying and designing new and even weirder configurations for 1987.

Many millions were spent this time round improving on Lexcen's idea. The most innovative designers took things many stages further. Tom Blackaller's *USA*, for example, had two rudders, one at the bow and one at the stern. Thus a rule framed in 1906 to maintain the status quo has ironically spawned one of the most intriguing developments in the history of racing yacht design.

CHAPTER THREE

A Game Played for High Stakes

Barry Pickthall

$200 million was a crazy sum to spend on a yacht race. Yet that was the conservative estimate of the amount invested in winning the America's Cup. Taking into account the services-in-kind provided to individual syndicates by government agencies around the world in research and promotional support, the figure probably ran closer to $300 million.

In the complex war to win the America's Cup, no stone was left unturned, and in the words of *Kookaburra III*'s skipper Iain Murray 'Turning over stones costs a heap of money'.

Advanced Aeromechanisms, Boeing, the California Institute of Technology, Ciba-Geigy, Cordtran, Cray Research, Chrysler, Digital, Grumman, the Massachusetts Institute of Technology, NASA, SAIC, Safe Flight Tractor Hydronautics and the University of Maryland; this formidable list reads like a file of Star Wars contractors, and in most cases that is correct. When the Cup was lost to a novel innovation, American syndicates thought that the know-how that had given Ben Lexcen's 'wing-keeled wonder' *Australia II* the edge against the traditional lines of the Dennis Conner-skippered *Liberty* would be simple enough for the mighty US to match and better.

'If we can send men to the moon, we can certainly improve on what Lexcen found out at the Dutch tank-testing facilities', was the arrogant response from one syndicate man soon after the Cup had been unbolted from its plinth in the New York Yacht Club.

What he didn't know was that a Dutch scientist, Dr Peter Van Oossanen, head of research at the Ship Model Basin in Holland, already held a 10-year lead in computerised design and tank-testing procedures, leaving the rest of the world with just two years to devise ways of leaping the technological gulf.

Even worse, the New York Yacht Club had ruled American syndicates out of tapping into this vital research source. Changes to the Deed of Gift governing the Cup races, drawn up by the Club several years before, barred foreign Challengers from using American technology by stipulating that Challengers could use foreign test-tank facilities only when their own country had no facilities of its own. Now the boot was on the other foot. Although the designer of *Liberty*, *France 3*, *Australia* and *Eagle*, Dutch émigré, Johan Valentijn, who has had more passports in his time than most MI6 spies during his clandestine efforts to design an America's Cup winner, crossed Dutch aerospace scientist Joop Sloof's palm for a copy of *Australia II*'s keel design, he got nothing more than the preliminary drawings. Sloof was the man who originally directed Lexcen's attention to a paper NASA had published on winglets.

The high hopes expressed by that syndicate spokesman might have rung true if Capitol Hill had treated the Cup's recapture with the same vigour it gave to President Reagan's Strategic Defence Initiative. He might also have been proved right if all the US syndicates had pooled their resources for research. Instead, they searched in five different directions and floundered amid reams of print-out paper. 'The Dutch have certainly left us with some catching up to do', said Bill Langan, chief designer at Sparkman and Stephens, the famous design office responsible for the three unsuccessful New York Yacht Club contenders *US 42, 44* and *46*, while enjoying a break from his drawing board during the 1985 SORC, adding, 'In this search for something new, it's all too easy to become overwhelmed with data.'

Leonard Greene's revamped *Courageous IV* was first to falter. Greene, head of Safe Flight Instruments Inc, had some innovative ideas for a keel, but refused to test them against *Australia II*'s, despite the fact that his British design co-ordinator Roger Marshall, now living near Newport, had copiously reproduced Lexcen's lines from measurements and photographs taken immediately after Alan Bond called for the shrouds to be pulled aside to reveal *Australia II*'s keel. 'That keel-shape failed because it created too much drag and insufficient lift', Dutch expert Dr Van Oossanen commented after the 13-year-old veteran design had been withdrawn, under an acrimonious cloud, without a win at the end of the first Round Robin Challenge Trials in October. 'Her trim tab was too large, her big fat wings were not set at anything like the correct dihedral angle and created huge vortices. Also, the vertical part of the keel was not big enough to stop leeway. *Courageous* had an almost perfect state-of-the-art hull form, and if the syndicate had bolted on almost any one of the 15 or more wing keels discarded around Fremantle by other groups, she would have finished half-way up the ladder.'

Dennis Conner's Sail America syndicate did as much as any of the US groups to turn up something new, but ended up with a boat so similar to Ben Lexcen's 1986 World Championship winner *Australia III*, that it belied the $4.2 million they spent on raw research. However, it all came right on the day.

Conner is a man of method, not inspiration. He builds up his own confidence by investing 250 days a year into sailing 12 Metres, leaving others to come up with the bright ideas. He is conservative in his thinking, leaving no stone unturned in testing one idea against another. Despite his unprecedented five-boat campaign to recover the Cup he lost in 1983, arch-rival Tom Blackaller's savage pre-race quote: 'It's just possible Conner's effort suffers from a lack of imagination' initially proved more perceptive than most people believed at the time.

Another to take a wrong turn somewhere along the design path was Johan Valentijn. He lacked little in technical back-up. Boeing provided their knowledge and computer expertise to develop the ultimate wing keel, and he enjoyed full use of Chrysler's powerful CAD/CAM (computer-assisted design/manufacturing) computer to analyse the stresses and engineer the yacht. Although his final models were tested at Offshore Technology Corporation's tank facilities at Escondido, California, he allowed his instincts complete rule over the final drawings. By his own admission, *Eagle*'s lines were never put to the test. She was designed to excel in medium winds and 'hang in there in a breeze' but in reality she never performed at all, the wild graphics depicting a bald-headed eagle painted down her topsides producing unkind comparisons with a turkey as the series wore on.

But Valentijn was by no means alone in choosing to ignore the result that these Star Wars computerised research tools can provide, for most designers continued to be sceptical of this new-found technology. The spectre of *Mariner*, the 1974 Britton

Chance design, built with a truncated bustle after tank-tests indicated that her underwater transom would cheat the water-flow into believing the boat was really longer than designed, still haunted some of the old hands, while others were simply overwhelmed by the myriad numbers spewed out by their computers.

The Graham & Schlageter designed *Heart of America* skippered by Buddy Melges proved no better, though a change of keel before the last Round Robin trials did have the effect of halving her deficits against the top boats.

The only American boat to show any real innovation was Gary Mull's radical twin-ruddered *USA II*, drawn with the aid of Dr Heiner Meldner, a nuclear physicist with expertise in fluid dynamics. Their design has a second carbon fibre rudder stationed close to the bow, developed to improve turning and share the work of the keel in limiting sideways drift or leeway.

Andrew Dovell, an engineer at the Offshore Technology Corp where *USA II* was tank-tested explained the canard rudder idea thus: 'It creates lift and changes the angle of attack for the keel. In addition it makes the boat more manoeuvrable. It's like a car, where both sets of wheels turn – that's the effect the canard has too.'

Other design groups to test the idea, including Conner's Sail America syndicate, and the Ship Model Basin in Holland, found that the forward rudder destroyed the water flow across the keel, but Mull and Meldner overcame this by hanging a simple torpedo-shaped lead bulb from one or more narrow aerofoil-shaped steel bars attached to the hull – its principal job being to act as a balancing weight and not provide anything like the lift wing keels generate. The one drawback to the *USA II* concept was the complex steering system which had metres of hydraulic hose-pipe and wire, linking the two foils. Also, according to Tom Blackaller, the two designers failed to agree on the variance in angles that the two rudders had to be set at. 'One insisted it should be six degrees, the other nine – and it cost us $400,000 and points during the first Round Robin series to find out which was wrong.'

Another problem he had to contend with was the total lack of 'feel' at the wheel, 'It's like flying a plane on instruments', the fast-talking Californian admitted. It made her a difficult boat to steer upwind. However it was obvious from the design's rapidly-improving form as the trials progressed that he got used to the boat's foibles. By late December she was looking more and more like a potential winner, although it was not to be.

Other Challengers
Like the Americans, the British and French were also forced to test their theories at home.

The Royal Thames Yacht Club chose to investigate two lines of thought – an evolutionary design drawn by Ian Howlett that merged *Australia II*'s winged-keel concept with the best attributes of his earlier *Victory '83* design built for millionaire Peter de Savary syndicate boss in 1983, and a radical design incorporating the ideas of model yacht architect David Hollom. Hollom, who had never designed a full-sized yacht before, was the syndicate's 'wild-card'. The innovative ideas he had presented to de Savary had anticipated Ben Lexcen's keel concept and cried out to be pursued. The Graham Walker-led British America's Cup Challenge gave him free rein, and working with two experienced designers, Stephen Wallis, head of Laurent Giles Ltd and Herbert Pearcey, a distinguished aeronautical designer specialising in fluid dynamics, between them they produced a boat that was certainly different. '*Hippo*', was her nickname in tribute to her unconventional underwater profile.

In early trials between the two boats, the Hollom design displayed dramatic but mysteriously inconsistent bursts of speed, proving particularly hard to keep in the groove. She was slower at tacking, an essential ingredient when match racing, and with both time and money in short supply, the team dropped the boat to concentrate their efforts on improving the Howlett design. In the end, a lack of development time, crewing mistakes and an unprecedented number of breakages – the tell-tale sign of lack of money – left the British effort just short of the points that would have taken them past the Semi-Final cut and instead, the team were back home by Christmas planning their next campaign – the 12 Metre World Championships in Sardinia. While the British tested their ideas in the tanks at the British Maritime Technology site at Feltham, the Wolfson unit at Southampton and the Royal Naval research establishment at Haslar, the French trusted in computer technology alone. The result of this work with plane makers Dassault and the French Space Research Centre (CNES) was *French Kiss*, an innovative Briand design with lines as Gallic as a Citroën 2-CV.

This boat showed considerable promise in the 1986 World Championships off Fremantle, winning two of the heavy-weather races, prompting others to copy her lines, despite the obvious French weakness in light airs. That problem was remedied in part by alterations in sail shape, and changing her delta-wing keel for a more radical Lexcen-styled upside-down foil with maximum width wings – fine tuning that was to lift this saucy French Challenge into the Semi-Finals against New Zealand's *KZ7*, later named *Kiwi Magic*.

The old adage that it takes a lengthy apprenticeship to do well in the America's Cup was buried by the performances of the Kiwis in the Challenge Trials and the equally impressive number of wins scored by the Iain Murray-skippered *Kookaburra III* – both first-time Challengers.

Not surprisingly perhaps, both turned in the first instance to the NSMB for testing and technical know-how. Money was tight at the start of the New Zealand campaign and Ron Holland, Bruce Farr and Laurie Davidson, the three-man design team responsible for the Kiwi glass-fibre 12 Metre had only a $10,000 budget to test their initial designs. The result was two identical boats that bore a marked similarity to *Australia II*, and after just nine days' practice, one of them, *KZ5*, skippered by 24-year-old sailing prodigy Chris Dickson, achieved the impossible by finishing second behind *Australia III* in the World Championships.

And that was just the start, for the result persuaded Kiwi patriotism into providing unlimited funding, allowing the design group to perfect their ideas at the Wolfson research unit at Southampton University. Was it the unique glass-fibre construction that made *Kiwi Magic* the boat to beat among the Challengers? 'No, that will have made little difference to stiffness or weight', Dr Van Oossanen said after the third Round Robin trials. 'Holland, Farr and Davidson are very bright designers, and between them, they have come up with a near-perfect hull form and very efficient wing keel.'

Not every group who tested their ideas out at the NSMB ended up with a winner, *Azzurra* and *Italia*, the two heavily-financed but disorganised Italian Challengers finished up near the bottom of the pile. '*Azzura II* proved fast in the tank but was then built with a keel that was too light and too small. Instead of increasing the size of the keel, the group chose to change the boat, commissioning two new designs to take to

Fremantle that were built too late to be tested. 'They left their best boat in Sardinia', Dr Van Oossanen recalled. The Yacht Club Italiano's campaign proved just as calamitous. *Italia*, their first boat, designed largely with the help of Ian Howlett, would have done better in the 1986 World Championships if her crew could have learned to stay aboard. *Italia II* was a considerable departure from the original British design, but testing and development came to a halt when the crane lifting her out of the water shortly after her launching, suddenly toppled over on top, sinking the boat and its chances.

However, the most extraordinary story from this intriguing series must come from the Eastern Australia Defence syndicate's *Steak'n'Kidney*, whose sudden change to competitiveness proved very embarrassing for designer Peter Cole. When the series began, the Sydney boat was the joke, not joker, among the Australian defence groups, all of whom had gone to NSMB to test their designs. The Cole design failed to take the winning gun in any of her first 20 races, but then came out at the start of the third Round Robin trials and walloped *South Australia* by more than five minutes.

To underline this new found form, *Steak'n'Kidney* led Alan Bond's *Australia IV* round seven marks only to lose at the finish when her genoa blew out, but to make up for the disappointment, her crew took *Kookaburra II*'s scalp the following week.

This sudden change of fortune came not from the chain-saw treatment other no-hope syndicates performed on the boats in last-ditch attempts to reach the Semi-Finals, but to the simple expediency of changing her keel.

Beforehand, syndicate boss Syd Fischer, who bank-rolled this Eastern Australian Challenger to the tune of $7m, was far from happy with his investment.

'You promised me a fast boat', the disgruntled hotel chain owner thundered down the phone at Van Oossanen in Holland. 'What went wrong?'

The Dutch scientist was just as perplexed. The Cole design had been tested with two different keels and proved significantly faster than the NSMB's bench-mark *Australia II*.

The answer came only when Van Oossanen paid a call to *Steak'n'Kidney*'s base in Fremantle. 'But that's the slow keel we tested, not the fast one' he exclaimed when looking at the boat hanging from her strops. In the rather heated discussions that followed, it emerged that the first keel, of a similar design to that of *French Kiss*, had been chosen because of the French boat's impressive performance in heavy weather during the World Championships.

'Syd just hit the roof', a close aide recalled. 'If Cole had had any money, he would have sued him for every cent'.

As it was, time was fast running out before the start of the second Round Robin trials, so Van Oossanen and Cole worked on producing a stop-gap replacement, re-modelling the existing plug into a more efficient shape and having this cast in time for the second series, before starting work on the new winged-keel that was to transform the yacht's performance. 'Improvements in keel design made up 70 per cent of the advances in this Cup series with the remainder split equally between electronics and rigs' Peter Van Oossanen confided.

Rigs
Compared with the mega-steps taken in the vertical-panelled sails the 40-year-old former nuclear physicist Tom Schnack-enberg developed for *Australia II*, now copied throughout the offshore racing world, developments in sail technology during this latest America's Cup were more subtle.

Schnack's efforts were a first (and very successful) attempt to align the strongest threads (warp) with the patterns of stress that build up within a sail, in an effort to reduce stretch to the very minimum. That concept was taken several steps further, almost trebling the number of panels within the sail, to produce a far stronger construction of the same weight.

The two French syndicates took this a step further, using the findings of a Government-backed aerospace research pro-gramme to develop their own sailcloth and testing facilities. Their cloth was the by-product of an abortive French/Russian project to launch a space probe to test the atmosphere around Venus. The joint venture called for a balloon to be launched from the Russian space rocket, made of a material strong enough to withstand the buffeting of 200 + mph winds known to cir-culate around the planet. When the project was cancelled, doubt-less as a result of the Afghan invasion, the lightweight laminated fabric developed by Brochier Espace and the machinery used to produce it, might well have been scrapped had not one of the research team, a keen boardsailor, made up a sail for himself from offcuts and found another use for this distinctive yellow coloured hi-tech cloth which, needless to say, is not available to anyone else.

Other syndicates experimented with various lightweight Mylar spinnaker fabrics. Initial experience with 0.4 oz 'see-through' ghosters suggested that these mylar sails would only be suitable over flat water, for in holding their shape better than nylon spinnakers, they tended to shake all the air out if seas were disturbed. That lesson led to two schools of thought when it came to developing heavier Mylar laminates. Some sail designers called for more elasticity, while others chose the most resistant laminates, believing that even if the sail was less forgiving, an experienced crew would get more out of a sail that always held its shape. Judging by the number of virgin white spinnakers flown during the Cup Trials, most syndicates chose the second route, though *Azzurra*'s crew was one to have continued experimenting along the more forgiving path, the wide-meshed nylon scrim laminated to the Mylar film making an almost transparent sail.

While Mylar/Kevlar laminate technology all but eliminated the bias stretch, the root cause of distortion in woven sails, producing ones that weighed and stretched less, their life-span still remains less than most boat-owners can afford.

Kevlar, the yellow synthetic fibre developed initially as a reinforcement for radial tyres, might have reduced stretch seven-fold but its stronger-than-steel properties degrade so quickly when bent, that any sail left to flog unnecessarily becomes tomorrow's sail-bag. A 12 Metre mainsail may cost $25,000, but its racing-life is little more than 30 hours. Little wonder therefore that headsails (which cost around $12,000) came shooting down the moment each boat crossed the finish line!

This led some sailmakers to pioneer latticework patterns of reinforcement across their sails to strengthen the principal lines of stress and limit the fibre deterioration and Mylar bond caused by the continuous flexing of the cloth. Horizon's distinctive 'Tape Drive' sails almost mirrored the three-dimensional stress analysis maps now generated on computer, while Sobstad's 'Strap-sail' approach provided a series of transverse 'X' patterns across the sails to maintain fore and aft shape. Sail shape was critical in this game. Each syndicate spent hours, days, months even, just speed-sailing in one direction against a trial-horse to perfect shape and setting.

Even when an optimum shape was found, the problem

became matching that shape exactly the next time those same conditions existed. Most syndicates kept a record of sheet and halyard tensions, but this made it almost impossible to take account of other small changes caused by breakages or replacements.

Kevin Parry's Taskforce '87 Defence syndicate, one of the highest-spending groups at Fremantle, with expenditure running at the rate of $40,000 a day, developed a unique digitised system of video cameras to provide a continuous record of sail shape. The four cameras – one at the masthead, two set either side of the hounds and the other sealed into the decks of both boats – were focused on three broad black 'shape' stripes traversing each sail horizontally close to spreader and hound heights. Analysing their telemetry test data and film after each day's sail, the group built up a database of optimum shapes which were then stored in graph form within the computer system onboard to be called up when required to provide a visible overlay to the live video pictures on display in the cockpit. Then, when the line followed by the shape stripes on the screen matched the graph lines, the trimmer knew that the particular sail was set to optimise the conditions.

Spars

One area of development that will doubtless provide immediate advancements in standard boat production is in the spars that carry these sails.

The higher wind speeds, bigger waves and stronger sails pressured all mastmakers to produce stiffer, stronger rigs than those stepped in Newport, without incurring a weight penalty.

One of the leaders in the field is Britain's Proctor Masts who provided 16 masts for seven syndicates – and seven of those to that all-conquering Challenger *Kiwi Magic* – which, at more than $75,000 apiece including boom and spinnaker poles amounted to quite an investment in itself.

Proctor's, whose managing director Richard Lang has links with the aerospace industry, harnessed the greater strength/weight ratios of hi-spec alloys developed for aircraft construction. Using 2014 coded alloy which provides a 60 per cent improvement in stiffness over the more general 6082 alloy used to extrude mast sections, their latest 2000 series masts had 7 per cent greater elasticity, and by chemically milling unwanted material out of the section in areas of low stress, customers were paying little more than a 5 per cent weight penalty – an amount more than compensated for by using titanium for gooseneck fittings and shroud tangs, cobalt steel for lower standing rigging and carbon fibre for jumpers and upper cap shrouds where wear from sail chafe is non existent.

The company also used Erfatyle plastic for sheaves, an extremely hard wearing copolymer that weighs less and stands up better than alloy to wire abrasion. Also new were their stainless ball-races – lighter than their more bulky alloy counterparts – that wear better and can be washed out with a hose.

Spreaders, the bulkiest of appendages on a mast, were smaller and lighter thanks to improved materials, and the use of carbon fibre in the manufacture of booms and spinnaker poles brought a 60 per cent weight saving.

Overall, rig developments during the past three years brought a significant improvement in strength while providing a 3–5 per cent overall weight saving, though naturally the price for this technology was heavy with a complete set of spars costing upward of $75,000.

But for all the money spent the gains in speed have been minute.

Seven years ago, 12 Metres were losing as much as 1.9 knots when they tacked. In 1983, *Australia II* reduced that loss to 1.2 knots, dropping from 8.2 down to 7 knots during turns, thanks to her keel and shallow bustle. Now the best Twelves go into a tack doing 8.5 knots and come out with their speed readings still registering 7.4 knots and enjoy tacking angles as close as 36 degrees apparent – a small return on a $200 million investment, one might think. But that's America's Cup racing – a game played for high stakes, where small increases in speed cost millions. It is a sobering thought that *White Crusader* needed only a 0.3 per cent improvement in performance to have made the Semi-Finals.

CHAPTER FOUR

Just Another Yacht Race?

Chris Freer

Significant events often occur so far backstage as to be overlooked even by the most acute observers; among the list must be a meeting held in America in November 1973 in a back room of the Mamaroneck Inn Diner. The subject under discussion concerned yet another Defence of the America's Cup, due to be held the following year. The difference which was to emerge between this and any other similar meeting in the Cup's long history was the fact that among the group there was a young man from San Diego, Dennis Conner, whose impact on the America's Cup scene was to be like no other.

Commodore George Hinman, veteran of several defences and a superb helmsman in his own right, was chairman of the newly formed Mariner syndicate. He represented the old school of the New York Yacht Club of which he had been a member for most of his life. Regarded as the ruling aristocracy of American racing, the Club had been responsible for producing most of the defenders in the preceding century and more and its committee and its attitudes reflected this background – the supervision of the defence by autocrats in a most democratic way. The new boy from San Diego cared little for tradition and viewed the '... clique of easterners in their red pants' as one of the burdens one had to bear if one were to be involved in yachting's premier competition. The difference between Conner and any man before him was that his will to succeed was all consuming. Not for him one short summer of honour and accolade and a place in history alongside victorious American skippers Harold Vanderbilt and Bus Mosbacher; Conner wanted to be recognised as the best in the world bar none and to achieve that meant turning his life over to the pursuit. In effect he embarked on a trail which would make him the first of a new breed of professional yacht racers, sounding the death knell to the Hinmans and serving notice that America's Cup yachting was about to become an even less gentlemanly sport.

Yachting was always the sport of the wealthy élite, but the style and structure of society has changed dramatically over the 136 years during which the America's Cup has been sailed. We shall never again see the likes of the industrial magnates: the Vanderbilts, the Sopwiths or the Liptons. The years of the last flowering of the Industrial Revolution backed by empire economies resulted in the generation of fabulous, virtually untaxed, wealth vested in the hands of individuals. Nations of workers toiled in support believing in their superiors and for the most part accepting their role.

Before the Second World War events like the Schneider Trophy races and the land speed record made use of the new media of radio and film newsreels to hold the public enthralled with a speed of communication unknown to the previous generation. This was a time for real, pure heroes and heroines like Lindbergh, Donald Campbell and Amy Johnson. In this atmosphere, a Challenge for the America's Cup was motivated by a mixture of an individual's sporting interest and national pride.

The Defence was no less a matter of national honour with the Americans evolving a satisfactory management solution very early on, with wealthy individuals or syndicates producing yachts in a spirit of intense competition. The races fitted well with the prevailing social atmosphere appropriate to the era of the Great Gatsby with the social élite of America and England meeting to compare notes on liner travel or business; the latter giving a hint of the future.

It was the 'King's grocer', Thomas Lipton, whose amiable features are seen on all the early newsreels who first realised that the America's Cup, coupled to the new communications provided a powerful and cheap advertising medium. Lipton's tea stormed America on the deck of a yacht. In this respect the advantage has always been with the Challenger and successive generations of astute businessmen have taken advantage of this unique social *entrée* into the world's richest consumer market. The top business families on the east coast of America were usually members of the New York Yacht Club, and Rhode

Island and nearby Cape Cod were their summer playgrounds. If New York and Boston were the centres of American business, then where better to make contacts?

Even in those pre-inflation days the cost of a J-boat campaign in 1937 was around £1 million, a figure that has only been exceeded recently by the 12 Metre syndicates. Of course if one takes the devaluation of currency into account then the incentive for change to smaller boats in the post-war period, when the world economies were flat, can be appreciated. That terrible war changed society in other ways than financial. There was a further reshaping of the social order and in the aftermath a process of social levelling was initiated in the western world which still continues.

It was 1956 before the America's Cup stirred interest in Britain and the name of the boat, *Sceptre*, together with the aristocratic nature of the Royal Yacht Squadron syndicate, recalled the images of the previous era. Even so it was clear that any Challenge or Defence would not have the benefit of the paid hands of previous days and would have to rely on volunteer amateur sailors with maybe a little help from the military. The Americans, less ravaged by war, always applied more money and expertise to these early 12 Metre series and were able to stay sufficiently far ahead to do the job, until sheer weight of numbers and persistence caught up with them. Strange that they would eventually be beaten on technical grounds; an area where they had always set the pace. Their reaction to the firm rumour regarding innovation was one of disbelief. If it wasn't American it couldn't be any good!

In times of peace man has always played war games. The peacetime wars are mainly in the boardroom or the stock market and it figures that the heroes and victors of these battles need a parade to receive the due accolade. In the modern world even the most gauche materialism has limits and in the struggle to display a success one must seek new arenas. The America's Cup competition is good in this respect. Socially elevating, sporting and comparatively reasonably priced, it not only focuses attention but provides contacts otherwise impossible.

The British had early on begun to consider that the Cup was their exclusive preserve, rather in the same way as they jealously guarded Mount Everest and the South Pole. A certain Australian ex-heavyweight boxer cum newspaper tycoon, Frank Packer, had, however, read the Lipton lesson and decided that America was the place to make contacts. Against the wishes of the British yachting establishment he muscled in on the action, disregarded the telegrams from the Royal Yacht Squadron and pressed on to gain accolade in Newport as a worthy, gutsy Challenger to whom the Americans could relate.

The close, well publicised 1962 Australian Challenge sparked world interest, sold lots of papers in Sydney, put the country on the map and Sir Frank in society. His *Gretel II* campaign of 1970 maintained the high standard of competition which has become an Australian hallmark and showed the world that the Yanks could be beaten.

Next to recognise that the route to the American market was through the doors of the New York Yacht Club was a French ballpoint pen manufacturer, Baron Bich. De Gaulle, the super nationalist, threw the full weight of a conscript army behind the Baron who promptly installed his first-born son in his American subsidiary to take the pen orders. In three magnificent and flamboyant campaigns Bich won the hearts of the two nations and sparked a yachting revolution in his home country. The French are now the premier yachting and yacht manufacturing nation of Europe. Liberty, equality and fraternity with world yachtsmen within a ten-year period was a quick return on the original investment.

Bond and Britain's Peter de Savary both campaigned in the accepted fashion, gaining probably more from business contacts than their campaigns ever cost in real terms. Bond was decent enough to stay at the table and play till he won the rubber; de Savary played a trump early on by wheeling in Prince Andrew, throwing a spectacular ball, then cashing in. Had he anticipated the size of the Perth event in commercial terms he might well have joined in; but then why put money up front to publicise Western Australian tourism?

The Cup could easily have died in 1983 when it was won by Bond because of the new level of expenditure neccessary to compete in Perth. No-one could guarantee that the Americans would be interested, but there was speculation that pride would force them to make at least a token effort. The 1983 Challenge series marked the gearchange between the new and the old orders. The entry of Dennis Conner changed the course of events by introducing a new standard of professionalism which would eventually overtake the rich individual owner. There was a desire to be free from amateurish interference in order to generate a new style of event run by professionals and funded by sponsors.

Starting in 1974 the Cup became the preserve of professional yachtsmen who used the event to build their business interests in an overt way. Conner's henchmen included such notables as Lowell North, Tom Blackaller and John Marshall. To these men the establishment of their world-wide sailmaking business interests was paramount. The Cup was just the pinnacle of events at which they had to succeed in order to dominate the sailmaking world. Many other marine companies now use the Cup series as their showroom and have invested heavily in the event's growth and expansion.

The sailing world now needs America's Cup racing as a publicity medium for the sport. The man in the street who probably knows little about yachting can relate to the two boat race, with a first-past-the-post winner, which no other form of yachting can really provide. Add a little bit of the old nationalism and a generous helping of publicity, throw in millions and millions of dollars and you begin to focus public attention.

But amid talk of all those millions it is as well to apply a little perspective. In 1986 a Chateau Lafitte bottled for Thomas Jefferson sold at auction for £105,000. The biggest art auction in the same year realised £42 million with a Rembrandt knocked down for £7¼ million. A golfer can earn $1 million in a year and a racehorse can cost four times that amount. Probably motor racing bears the closest comparison with the aspirations of yachting because it has comparable technology. With Marlboro paying a minimum of £1 million a year to each of four grand prix drivers and qualifying tyres burning at the rate of £2000 a lap, one can only speculate on the secret total budget of a top team.

So when we hear that sails cost $1 million for a two-year campaign and that an English America's Cup helmsman earns about £25,000 in a year for his efforts we are talking peanuts in world sporting terms.

What has emerged in Perth is a multi-million pound tourist and publicity industry which can be won as first prize for a yacht race. It's like giving the Olympic Games to the town which can win the most gold medals . . . except that the yachting has become a potentially richer prize and it lasts longer. No expensive stadiums to build either. It is worth millions to the nation in tourism and world publicity and it is small wonder that a country like New Zealand, with its siege economy, can see the potential of winning.

So it is hooray for Alan Bond, Benbob (Ben Lexcen) and 'Aero' Bertrand, the team that won the Cup in 1983. If they hadn't come along, the 'super circus' in Perth would never have happened and the New York Yacht Club would still be sitting on top of the sport administering affairs with all the sparkle of a Victorian funeral parlour.

A little problem always crops up when a sport breaks with its amateur tradition and the players start earning enough to have a voice. Frank Packer's son Kerry understood this when he turned the cricket establishment on its head in the 1970's. The same has occurred in motor racing, equestrian events and even darts. The question is, do the establishment who have nurtured and protected the sport for the many years prior to D-Day fight a rearguard action and die like heroes or do they regroup, jump ahead, and take over the emergent monster? Yachting authorities are at last facing this decision. The result will affect yachting of all classes on a world-wide basis.

It is the International Rule 26 forbidding advertising on yachts which has at last come under proper siege in Perth. The ruling aristocracy have been fighting a rearguard action over sponsorship and professionalism for years and they and the major authorities and yacht clubs have been responsible for policies which have retarded the growth of the sport. Rule 26 in its old restrictive form hurt the interests of participants and the industry, as well as those of the public at large who have a right to general sports coverage.

In Perth we have seen what a bit of cash and a correct media attitude can do. Cameras on board the boats brought pictures of racing unknown except to the crew. Regular coverage established personalities, a very necessary part of any public interest sport. Even so how many sports watchers appreciated that Cadillac and Newsweek are sponsors of American boats? Or that White Horse Whisky were behind the British? So even after modification the rule is still couched in terms unlikely to prove attractive to sponsors because of a lack of definition. It is obvious that the TV cameras and sponsors require the advertising to be writ large on the yacht and its sails, not restricted to postscript size labels.

The Mensheviks, the élite wealthy amateurs, have always appeared frightened of professionalism, knowing that they will be shown up as wanting in skills when the revolution comes. In the process these 'princes' have nearly sounded the death knell for their own sport. In the last decade the level of racing competition has increased hand in hand with the expensive materials required to create faster yachts. This escalation has taken the racing yacht into an exciting but incredibly costly area, unattainable and unattractive to the ordinary yachtsman.

The multi-million dollar road show that should result from the activities in Perth will be the best thing to happen in yachting this century. With any luck there will be several grands prix in different venues each year, all correctly sponsored and attractive to the media. The first event takes place in Sardinia in June and July 1987 and it shows every sign of becoming a great success paving the way for other venues. All this activity will build up to the America's Cup series, hopefully hosted by a different country every three years. A truly exciting prospect for sports aficionados world wide. Just another yacht race? No longer.

CHAPTER FIVE

The Englishman, the Irishman and the Hippo

Tim Jeffery

If spending £6 million over three years in an America's Cup bid could be considered anything other than totally serious, then the more light-hearted might like to hear the tale of the Englishman, and the Irishman plus their friends the Admiral and the *Hippo*.

For these four were the components of Britain's 19th Cup Challenge since *America* beat the best of the British fleet around the Isle of Wight in 1851. In common with the previous 18 Challenges, this one failed too.

The Englishman in this latest tale of apparent woe is Graham Walker, a Jersey-based millionaire who has worked hard for much of his life and who is now enjoying playing very hard. He recruited the Irishman, Harold Cudmore, a sailor of the highest calibre who fortunately for British sailing enjoys dual nationality. This oddity is a throw-back to Lloyd George's highly refined sense of political expediency which led him to grant British nationality to all Irish people and their children when Ireland was partitioned and separated from Britain.

The *Hippo* was the nickname given to one of the 12 Metres built for the challenge: a radical, ungainly boat which showed erratic speed and which was sidelined in favour of a more conventional boat, *White Crusader*.

And then there was the Admiral. He was the epitome of the type considered high on the list of undesirables onboard sailing yachts, ranking high alongside objects such as umbrellas and grand pianos. Yet Admiral Sir Ian Easton had one overwhelming virtue. He was the man who lodged the Challenge. If it wasn't for the enterprise of a man who had previously only a passing interest in sailing, Britain would have not been involved in the biggest, most expensive, most technologically advanced America's Cup series since its inception.

It was an incredibly close run thing, however. With the deadline set by the Royal Perth Yacht Club of 31 March 1984 looming, Admiral Easton thought it inconceivable that Britain should not be represented. His motives were as simple as that, and with less than three days to go for the Challenge to be made he tried to find other like-minded individuals. So the Challenge which was to be played out on the other side of the world began in Yarmouth, the pretty harbour town at the western end of the Isle of Wight. There the Admiral met John Foot, rear commodore of the Royal Thames Yacht Club aboard the latter's rather splendid 44 ft yacht *Water Music IV*. Foot gave his support to the Easton plan but needed to refer the Challenge idea to the club's sailing committee.

Though America's Cup sailing is nothing short of a battle of business organisations these days, Challenges are still lodged in the time-served fashion through yacht clubs. The Royal Thames first went down that path in 1870 when James Ashbury's *Cambria* attempted, but failed, to avenge America's win in 1851 and more recently in 1964 with Tony Boyden's equally unsucessful *Sovereign*.

Not surprisingly, the Thames was circumspect. It had its reputation as one of the world's oldest and most senior yacht clubs (founded in 1775) to consider. Its membership may not read like Debretts, as is the case with the Royal Yacht Squadron at Cowes, but HRH the Prince of Wales is the commodore. The clubhouse itself is at the smart end of Knightsbridge, opposite Harvey Nicholls, one of the bars is named the 'Quarterdeck' and the walls are adorned with portraits and memorabilia from royal yachts. The Thames has a cachet which few yacht clubs anywhere in the world can match.

But the Thames' committee faced more than a deadline. There was a complication in the shape of Peter de Savary, the Bahamas-based businessman who had bankrolled the *Victory* Challenge in 1983. Despite acrimonious crew hiring and firings, a flamboyant leadership which saw Aston Martins, seaplanes and a one time Elizabeth Taylor/Richard Burton motor yacht used as a floating headquarters, the Challenge had achieved far more than just de Savary's self-advancement. The British boat *Victory '83* was the only one to come close to matching *Australia*

II which went on to win the Cup.

De Savary and his partner, public relations man Kit Hobday, were also keen to have another crack and wanted the Royal Thames' backing. The club which had sponsored the *Victory* Challenge, the Royal Burnham Yacht Club in Essex, did not want to have a second try.

While these machinations were going on behind closed committee room doors, Admiral Sir Ian Easton also had to find the $10,000 deposit the Royal Perth Yacht Club would require with any Challenge and a Navy pension wasn't going to be enough. But as a former commandant of the College of Defence Studies in London and our Defence Attaché in Washington, he had powerful friends.

One was another retired Admiral, Sir Raymond Lygo, head of British Aerospace. He had noted that the National Aerospace Laboratory in the Netherlands had helped in developing *Australia II*'s novel winged keel. Suddenly yacht designers were keen to absorb aerospace companies' expertise so he agreed to provide the deposit cheque and technical support if Admiral Easton could get the Royal Thames to give the project the green light. They did and the telex was sent to Western Australia with hours to spare.

Sir Ian Easton already had one possible designer in mind. Ornithologist and amateur aerodynamicist Warwick Collins had come up with the idea of a keel-in-front-of-a-keel. Called a Tandem keel, it had raced successfully in the Solent underneath a hull designed by Laurent Giles. Collins thought this novel wing form would work on a 12 Metre. Warwick Collins did not stay with the embryonic British Challenge to find out if it did, though Stephen Wallis of Laurent Giles did. He brought with him the experience of working on the design of *Victory* which Ed Dubois created for Peter de Savary back in 1981/82.

While Wallis had practical 12 Metre experience behind him as well as naval architecture qualifications, the Admiral was canvassed by someone else who lacked both. He was David Hollom, a Yorkshireman and former salesman who had developed intense interest in model yachts during his days away from home in the Merchant Navy.

In fact Hollom had become a highly accomplished scale yacht designer. His boats had won many championships and he had been involved with a project, code-named Acorn, which de Savary had funded to explore radical ideas for 12 Metres in model form. While *Australia II* was being created secretly in the computers and towing tank of the Netherlands Ship Model Basin, Hollom had produced a design called Royal Oak for Project Acorn. In the world of model yachts where fanciful ideas are commonplace, the boat looked ordinary enough; when scaled up to the size of a real America's Cup yacht, a 65 ft yacht, it was outrageous.

Few took him seriously despite his having written in *Yachting World* about why winged keels would work, months before *Australia II* won the Cup in sensational fashion and her unusual underbody was revealed.

That win convinced Hollom that he was on the right track and he phoned, wrote to and cajoled anyone and everyone who looked as if they were in the next America's Cup game in 1987. On his list was Admiral Sir Ian Easton.

Things were beginning to shape up. Hollom and Wallis formed a team. The Admiral deployed his powers of strategic planning. Money had to be raised (lots of it), a skipper found (an excellent one) and the whole campaign had to take on a form and structure.

From the very outset money proved to be a problem. Fund raisers came and went. First West-Nally, the sports promotion company in which cricket commentator Peter West has an interest and who put together an impressive consortium for the Italian Azzurra group, then IMP, a subsidiary of the D'Arcy, MacManus & Masius advertising agency.

Still no big catch could be landed. Names like Tate & Lyle and Trafalgar House were linked with the Challenge but none signed a contract. Only British Airways were persuaded to put up £250,000, a sum which proved invaluable in shifting personnel to and from Perth.

Among those knocking on boardroom doors, trying to succeed where the professional fund raisers had failed was Harold Cudmore who came aboard as skipper. Under a far-reaching agreement, the campaign effectively became his. He was the Sailing Director, responsible for taking the key design, equipment and crew decisions. As the lynchpin of the executive team he was involved in every other pertinent decision as well. Having resigned from the de Savary campaign Cudmore didn't want it any other way. As one of the few people in the rarified world of global grand prix sailing, Cudmore has few equals when it comes to combining and optimising the many elements required to produce a winning effort. What he was taking on for the 1987 America's Cup was equivalent to starting a brand new Formula One team, managing it and driving the car himself. Few doubted that he could do it.

The Irishman arrived on the international sailing scene in 1974 at Cowes Week. Sailing *Alouette de Mer*, he chalked up a few wins in a cruiser racer. Previously, Cudmore had enjoyed a comfortable Cork background, strong on cruising and dinghy racing. But from 1974 onwards he had competed with increasing success. In 1976 when the Irish Yachting Federation declined Harold's late bid to make the Flying Dutchman Class selection in the Irish team for the Olympic regatta in Canada, Harold bounced back by rush-building a half tonner called *Silver Shamrock*, towing it across Europe to Trieste behind a tired and reluctant Jaguar and winning the Half Ton Cup. To celebrate his win, Cudmore nipped across the top end of the Adriatic Sea and went crusing in Venice, sailing his world champion racing yacht up the Grand Canal. Above all, Cudmore showed extraordinary ability at the unusual form of competition used in the America's Cup, match racing, where one boat meets another. Match racing requires intimate knowledge of the yacht racing rules and how they can be exploited to advantage, quite apart from normal yacht racing skills of boat handling and wind and tide strategy.

Cudmore's arrival gave the British effort some direction. His extrovert character made him the obvious focus of attention, something of which the self-effacing Admiral clearly approved.

As a sailor, he is very intense, achieving high levels of concentration by constant chatter. He's been compared to a James Joyce figure whereby his consciousness brings thoughts at the back of his mind constantly to his lips. He has a zest for life which stimulates those who can match his pace and exhaust those who cannot.

The Admiral also managed to add another designer to the group, Ian Howlett, who had created Britain's two previous Challengers: *Lionheart* (1980) and *Victory '83*. Howlett did not join the team immediately for two reasons. First, he was on a long-standing retainer from Peter de Savary and secondly he was working for the Yacht Club Italiano group on a consultancy basis, helping the design house of Giorgetti & Magrini get to grips with 12 Metres for their first time.

Howlett could not be more different to Hollom. A Balliol

graduate, Howlett had made 12 Metres his life. He liked to work alone from his New Forest cottage in Beaulieu with forays to the test tank at the Wolfson Unit in Southampton and at Royal Navy Haslar in Portsmouth. His past experience and world-wide reputation led many to believe that Howlett's boat for 1987 would be competitive. The Admiral saw the boat as the group's insurance policy, a design good enough to compete with 21 other groups which had expressed initial interest in challenging from five countries.

Meanwhile, Hollom and Wallis were working on the *Hippo*, the radical 12 Metre which would be the British gamble. If the unusual configuration worked, the British would have a boat like no other and only they would know why it worked. The Hollom/Wallis team was boosted by the presence of Herbert Pearcey, an eminent aero- and hydrodynamicist. A film maker would have typecast Pearcey as the 'Boffin', a tag which would have stuck when they found out that he had designed the supercritical wings of the Harrier Jump-jet as well as several British civilian airliners. But Pearcey was also the former head of research at BMT (British Marine Technology), one of the world's leading test tank facilities with buildings at Teddington and Feltham. Hollom and Wallis were soon to begin testing their one-tenth scale models in the very same tank as Barnes Wallis developed the war-time bouncing bomb. As their ideas refined, they moved on to third scale models in the quarter-mile-long tank, towing the miniature 12 Metres up and down at different angles of heel, yaw and with various degrees of rudder and trim tab (a second rudder) to study speed potential and wave-making (i.e. drag) characteristics. It was the same painstaking and unglamorous work Ian Howlett was doing on his design.

Because high technology had won the Cup for the Aussies, British Aerospace were keen to continue their support by allowing use of their computers at BAe Brough up on Humberside. But it was a computer flow programme at BMT, written by George Gadd, which ultimately proved more useful for studying hull form and keel shapes, together with the wind tunnel at City University.

While Howlett produced the conventional style yacht expected of him, Hollom's original Project Acorn design survived all the technology that was thrown at it. When it was revealed, or at least partially revealed at launch time and studied from the air when sailing, it became clear that the *Hippo* was aptly named. It had a big bulbous chin just below the waterline forward. At its after end, the hull fined out to a long chisel stern while underneath was slung a tiny keel with an enormous flattened lead torpedo to give the yacht stability.

Although BMT and British Aerospace had helped support the British challenge in kind, it was clear that someone was paying the bills behind the scenes. In the absence of commercial sponsors other than British Airways, that someone was the Englishman in our story, Graham Walker. Without him, the British challenge would quite simply have fizzled out. It was Walker who kept it fuelled with funds.

Not that Graham Walker was overkeen to broadcast that fact. Despite playing at the highest levels of sailing, this tall, big-framed man from the north-west has no overwhelming sense of self-importance. In fact, you would be hard pressed to find a bigger contrast to Peter de Savary whose previous British campaign was high-profile with a capital H and capital P.

While Walker signed the cheques, the designers got on with their unglamorous, unseen work in the test tanks, wind tunnels and computers.

Although the Admiral had been looking for a front man for almost as long as he had set the British Challenge off on its road to Fremantle, he himself suddenly became fair game for the Fleet Street gossip columnists. After all, they reasoned, if the Admiral was heading a challenge through Prince Charles' 'own' yacht club and the Princess of Wales was going to name the 12 Metre, then his private life should be brought into the public domain.

But they paid little attention to Graham Walker. It was his private life, especially a very serious car accident to his son Max, which kept Walker out of the limelight. It was only at the London Boat Show in January 1985 that Walker emerged from the wings as the man whose money Harold Cudmore was spending.

At 46, Graham Walker had made such a success of his business that he had left the Wirral for the sunnier shores of Jersey and was able to devote time and funds to sport. A self-made son of a policeman, Graham Walker is the antithesis of the brash, *nouveau riche* stereotype southerners label successful northerners. Walker has a commanding presence, not so much due to his physical attributes as an easy and persuasive charm which seems to keep a perpetual twinkle in his eyes.

Walker has always been a sportsman. He played rugby at school and captained New Brighton RFC before launching into sailing in 1978 as a way of growing old gracefully. It's typical of the man that the plan to buy a boat was hatched in a pub but the ever-competitive Walker decided if he was going sailing he might as well spend the money, get the best and have a crack at the top honours. His first yacht, *Indulgence*, came close to winning the Half Ton Cup. Walker's skipper Phil Crebbin, then a successful dinghy and keelboat sailor, was finally to join Cudmore as one of key decision makers in the British 12 Metre challenge. Walker followed that up with a succession of *Indulgences*, all of which sailed in world championships or prestigious events such as the Admiral's Cup at Cowes. He was rewarded by being made British Admiral's Cup captain in 1983 and by sailing the top yacht *Phoenix* in the 1985 Admiral's Cup. His campaign was run by Harold Cudmore who needed just such a boost to reinforce his claim of being the best sailor-manager in the world. The yacht's helmsman was Eddie Warden Owen.

Were any endorsement of Walker's persuasive power needed then ask Willie Gilbertson-Hart. He was driving his rare and desirable 1926 3-litre Red Label Bentley along in north Wales when he was flashed, pursued and finally forced off the road by the driver of a Range Rover. It was Walker. He wanted the car and offered to swop on the spot with a cash adjustment. Within 15 minutes Walker had made another conquest.

Walker's biggest conquest, however, was selling the idea of booze and cigarette counters in supermarkets. At the time he worked for brewers Greenall Whitley who didn't like the idea so Walker went off and did it himself, to become a pioneer in selling alcohol and tobacco in supermarkets when aged 30. By the early 1970s Walker had 350 concessions and was turning over £100 million. His North-West Vintners became a public company called Amalgamated Distilled Products which in turn was bought by James Gulliver's Argyll Group, owners of Presto supermarkets. Argyll v Guinness was THE big take over battle of 1986 and although Argyll lost, its standing and share price in the City was heightened. Walker is both a non-executive director and major shareholder. Moreover it brought Walker and others involved in the British Challenge into close contact with Ernest Saunders, chief executive of Guinness, the man who took the plunge and signed a £1 million sponsorship deal with the British in September 1986. Actually the deal cost Guinness less than £1 million for it was by instalments, with more money becoming available as the British advanced through the elimination series. But it did ensure that after two years of running on a shoe-string, the British had money during the most important months of competition. Guinness was not only promoting its White Horse Whisky brand by backing the British effort but had also thrown in another huge sum to the Royal Perth Yacht Club to become the 'official' whisky of the America's Cup.

But despite this, and a share issue in the spring of 1985, Walker remained the principal angel behind this particular production, with a personal input of £1.3 million. The Englishman has always called this an investment. In a sense he is right for under the terms of the share issue, made under the Business Expansion Scheme, the shares of British America's Cup Challenges Plc have to be traded for at least three years. Also, the company was deliberately named Challenges, plural not singular, as Walker and Cudmore are in this long-term. The 1987 bid was not just a one-off. If the British were ever to win, BACC hold the rights to stage and market the Cup, a mini-industry in itself, now valued at £1 billion.

Nevertheless, the Englishman has consistently refused to become a centre-stage figure like Alan Bond or Michael Fay of the Kiwi challenge. He left the spotlight to the Irishman, Cudmore, and even to the Admiral to some extent and that certainly wasn't in Sir Ian Easton's long-term strategic plan. . . .

The first fruits of the designers' efforts were born in late 1985. Cougar Marine of Hamble, creator of Richard Branson's ill-fated *Virgin Atlantic Challenger 1*, built both British 12 Metres. Ian Howlett's boat was first to be finished, a clean looking wholesome yacht. Compared with his previous *Victory '83* design, *Crusader 1* appeared to have more flared bow sections to add buoyancy in the bigger Australian seas, the maximum beam further aft and a cut-away bustle at the after end of the underbody.

The Princess of Wales named the yacht and the 12 Metre was taken to the London Boat Show in January 1986. This move was a calculated risk. Despite the launch of BACC which had raised £3 million the British Challenge were still looking for another £2 million plus so the boat was put before the British boating public. True to form the public and business community showed a singular lack of interest. The downside of this public relations exercise was that it delayed the boat's arrival in Fremantle. Delays in starting its building had ruled out competing in the 12 Metre World Championships, although Harold Cudmore did manage an appearance with a skeleton British/French crew aboard the outclassed *Challenge 12*. It at least permitted a firsthand look at the new generation 12 Metres sailing in the new venue but it was a last minute snatched opportunity. It, emphatically, was not the start of the British work-up in Australia, something that did not happen until June 1986, some five months later.

Up until then you could have faulted the British Challenge even though it was hampered by a sponsoring club which never looked fully committed to the Challenge carrying its name. It was hardly surprising at this stage that others did not share their confidence. But missing the World Championships and letting the timetable slip was something the Irishman, Englishman and Admiral would surely have preferred to avoid.

Some thought their salvation might come in the form of the *Hippo*, Britain's second, radical boat which arrived in July. The hope was that even if the British were short of time and funds then perhaps those disadvantages could be wiped off by an excess of boat speed from a design which other groups did not have and could not copy successfully in time.

From her brief launching in England prior to shipping the clues were all there that the *Hippo* was a blown-up version of one of Hollom's Project Acorn designs. Despite a full tank-test programme, other refined design aids and input from Herbert Pearcey, Hollom's model yacht ideas surfaced in full size in a recognisable form. Being a newcomer, Hollom felt no inhibitions of accepted wisdom. Because hull length above the water was not a component in the rule, *Hippo* or *Crusader 2*, had a long stern which would add sailing length upwind when the yacht heeled or when she surfed down waves when reaching and running. Because stability is free in the rule, Hollom went for as much of that as possible by placing a long torpedo-style lead bulb on the end of a narrow, swept-back keel. The only real difference that the layman would spot between *Crusader 2* and Hollom's model Twelve was the big bulbous chin just under the waterline forward. Just like big ships have bulbs, so Hollom and his cohorts found that the bigger the bulb they added to the canoe body the less resistance it made slipping through the black waters of the NMI test tanks.

When the two yachts sailed together in Australia it was not immediately evident which was superior. *Crusader 1* moved well, tacked quickly and seemed a pretty good all-rounder on most points of sail and in most conditions. If she had a fault it was of pronounced weather helm which was initially cured by cutting the mainsails with less area in the roach. *Crusader 2* on the other hand took more sorting out. Her trim and balance weren't quite right. Internal ballast was shifted and the boat could be fast upwind and slow downwind one day while being the opposite the following day. More worrying was that she had lee helm, something that the soft-leeched mainsail cut for $C1$ did nothing to help. Also the mast could not be moved back further to help sort out the problem because the assumed wisdom in 12 Metres has always been that masts have to go forward if a balance problem exists, but $C2$ was atypical.

What was clear was that $C2$ proved slow to turn. To tack she required a different technique. Normally the helmsman on a Twelve moves the trim tab from, say, two degrees upwind to two degrees downwind just before a tack so that the keel is generating maximum lift straightaway on the new tack. To tack, the wheel is simply put over. On $C2$ however, she needed both rudder and trim tab to be turned in unison to steer the boat through the tack. Sailed this way she could keep up with $C1$ in a tacking duel before losing ground. Despite this $C2$ did have one unusual characteristic. She was able to hang head to wind for long periods without falling off onto one tack or the other – a useful ploy when trying to assert control over the rival yacht in the pre-start period of a match race.

Sadly, it seems, $C2$ was never in her optimum configuration during the three days intensive trials held in early September 1986 to decide which boat to use. Her mainsails were cut for $C1$, her trim tab gearing needed altering and her mast needed moving aft. Even then she looked competitive to outside observers such as the Royal Yachting Association's women's and youth squad coach Jim Saltonstall, particularly in winds 20 knots plus with a bit of sea running.

Perhaps another two months would have made the difference. Whatever, Harold Cudmore and his two helmsmen Chris Law and Eddie Warden Owen thought that the conservative $C1$ was the better of the two. In any case Cudmore had gone on the record very early on with his views on 'breakthrough designs':

'I am very conservative when it comes to choosing boats. I am confident enough in my own ability to ask for only an equal boat.' With those words the Irishman put the *Hippo* out to grass.

In October the Irishman's skills and those who had grouped around him were put on the line in the first race of the Challenger eliminations: the first round to see which of 13 boats from five countries would win the right to race the Aussies for the America's Cup.

Cudmore had searched high and low for his crew. 'The standard in 12 Metres is so high that Admiral's Cup sailing is almost an irrelevance to the standard I will require ultimately', he said. 'You have boats which don't stay in the groove. You need trimmers who can engineer sail shapes in seconds. How many people would you trust in a £1 million sail programme? You ask these hard questions and you come up with tough answers', explained Cudmore about just one of the responsibilities resting upon him.

He took crew from the grand prix circuit: Swiss trimmer Michel Maedar, sail coordinator and reserve helmsman Eddie Warden Owen, mastman Mel Coleman. He took veterans from the *Victory* campaign such as mainsheet trimmer Chris Mason and grinder Mark Preston or Whitbread Round the World race veterans such as bowman Paul Standbridge, or their Olympic dinghy and keelboat sailors such as helmsman Chris Law and trimmers Jerry Richards and Mike McIntyre. And there were maxi-boat sailors such as Louis Rich from *Kialoa*. And finally where sustained stamina were required ahead of sailing skill there were the big men, the grinders who toiled on the handles which powered the trimmers' winches. There was world class oarsman Clive Roberts and the men who won their right for nine months' hard labour by winning the *Daily Mail* Winchman competition – Alexis Bisbas, Paul Rushent and Sean Campbell.

At the beginning of the trials things looked good for the British Challenge. Harold Cudmore lived up to his reputation by winning virtually all the starts. The shore support group pulled their weight. Our Proctor masts, featuring a new type of high strength/low weight aluminium alloy were highly refined. They were supported by cobalt rod rigging and matched the sails designed by Angus Melrose, one of the world's top 12 Metre sail designers. Better still, our harbour compound in Fremantle was effectively a mini boatyard. It might not have had the air-conditioned offices of the New York Yacht Club's compound or the Astroturfed hospitality balcony belonging to the Kiwis but it did have a shed big enough to wheel *Crusader* straight in, a squad good enough to undertake major work on her, and sufficient floor space to build sails on site using a computer-controlled plotter and cutter.

It was a formidable operation, equivalent to a Formula One team setting up its design, manufacture and repair facility right by the race track. And the British had one of the best while spending a quarter of what the other top groups did.

Of the many elements which make up a winning campaign – top skipper, top helmsman, good crew, good hull, good sails, backed by sufficient resources and an organised management – it looked as if the British had got most areas right. Moreover the calibre of the key decision makers was such that the numerous small judgments that have to be made about the mix of ingredients to find the small gains which put a good Challenge on top was adequate.

But it did not stop things going wrong, to such an extent that a Challenge which had looked good enough to be in the Semi-Finals failed to make the cut. As ever, yacht races boil down to what happens on the race course and people who sail the yachts. In Round Robin 1, where wins scored just one point, *White Crusader* retired from a race when her mast buckled. The inquest showed Cudmore had taken a gamble by crash gybing in strong winds. This was enough to whip the slack standing backstay, explode a block in it and transfer the load to the safety strop which is fitted to the backstay for those occasions when a yacht passing behind misjudges distance and puts her bow over the other yacht's transom, so hooking out the backstay. During the crash gybe, this strop suddenly brought up the mast, whipping like a fishing rod, and causing it to buckle.

In Round Robin 2, the boom broke, a result again of aggress-ive sailing in hard, tough conditions. *White Crusader* was batt-ling just behind the fast-improving *French Kiss*, sailing by the lee attempting to take the inside berth at the leeward buoy. Then she buried her bow in *French Kiss's* quarter wave stopping the boat abruptly. Inertia kept the rig moving forward at 10 knots until it too stopped suddenly a fraction later. The loads from the hull passed into the rig, up the hydraulic vang to the boom which crumpled at the attachment point. The inquest showed that the mainsheet trimmer was on the handles of the pedestal, not holding the tail of the sheet. If he had, it's possible he could have caught the slack in the sheet and dampened the snatch on the boom. The boom also showed that two fail-safe sacrificial links in the boom vang which should have broken before the whole vang overloaded did not do their duty. It was a bit like a fuse failing to blow and save the whole ring. You could say that the inquest's verdict was one of misadventure.

But *White Crusader* lost other races too, fatally against *America II* and *New Zealand*, by now called *Kiwi Magic*, by six and three seconds when she was fighting for her life in Round Robin 3. Then there was no gear failure, no breakages, just the inability to break the line vital inches ahead of her rival.

It was those seconds, those inches which cost *White Crusader* a Semi-Final place as much as catastrophic breakages and fast-improving rival yachts.

Even the major changes to hull between Round Robin 2 and Round Robin 3 (which saw essentially subtle alterations of the keel to make it lower, of the bow to make it higher and drier and of the rudder to ease the amount of helm pressure) were not enough to find that elusive fraction of extra speed which could have turned losses into wins.

In her final configuration of altered hull and second keel sporting their third set of wings, *White Crusader* was a competitive boat. Perhaps the new, third keel, would have added the extra cutting edge of more sail area for the same stability. But time finally ran out and at the end it was that essential ingredient which the British lacked more than anything else. In the words of Chris Law:

We got bloody close. It was a nauseatingly *British* effort – a brave try, but lacking in the professionalism of say the Kiwis.

The tactics and steering were never under attack – it was in other areas that we fell down. Nobody could have steered the boat better and there was no better tactician than Harry, but we would have been hard pushed to beat *Stars & Stripes* and the Kiwis.

Because of our late start we were 2–3 months behind. No matter how hard we tried we could not afford to miss a start or break anything. But look at our rate of climb against the Kiwis. Four minutes, then one and a half and then six seconds. In the last race against the Kiwis we raced as perfectly as we could. Even though they gave us a minute during that race they had speed to burn. They outcrewed us. Sooner or later they would have beaten us.

We started late, but at least we paid our bills and above all treated people properly. It would be a shame to see it all fall by the wayside.

The lack of time could have been made up for if we had had a breakthrough boat. As it was *White Crusader* was a superb conventional boat. Our radical boat couldn't beat it. The programme was good. Harry is very good conceptually. It was right to have had a benchmark boat for the radical option. Without C_2 there would have been no programme, but in the end we were beaten by four radical boats. We were the best of the conventional boats.

The epitaph for a challenge started by an Admiral, bankrolled by an Englishman and sailed by an Irishman was, as ever, 'too little too late'.

CHAPTER SIX

What the Papers Said

Stuart Alexander

Speculation surrounding any America's Cup bid invariably makes fascinating reading after the event, and this was as true for the British Challenge in 1986 as it had been for all the other unsuccessful attempts over the 136-year history of the event.

The Press, so often over-confident about the prospects of a home win, were at first muted. Having hyped Peter de Savary's 1983 campaign, only to see it founder when *Victory '83* was beaten by *Australia II*, they were in a bet hedging mood; torn between outright support and cynical dismissal. And they can hardly have been blamed, as it happened.

Nevertheless, when on 10 April 1984 the Royal Thames Yacht Club announced that it would challenge for the Cup, and that they were backing a syndicate organised at the last minute by retired Admiral Sir Ian Easton, over a rival bid by de Savary's old right-hand man Kit Hobday, the Press interest was immediate.

It mattered little that the February issue of the specialist magazine *Yachts and Yachting* had already dismissed any de Savary involvement. What possible interest could the elusive Bahamas-based millionaire have in Western Australia, 'Where is the money to be made in Western Australia?', asked the magazine. 'Come to think of it, where is Western Australia?'

Even as the Royal Thames took its final decision on the last day for an entry to be lodged, the *London Standard* reported that de Savary was on the verge on making his own decision to join the 21 entries received by the Royal Perth Yacht Club. If de Savary – friend of royalty, quoter of quotable quotes was involved – that was news.

And yet Bob Ward, Secretary of the Royal Thames, was still not sure if there was a British Challenge at all, let alone one involving de Savary. On the eve of the deadline he said: 'To the best of my knowledge there is no solid British entry as yet. There is only one possibility . . .'.

The 'holding' Challenge duly lodged, the Press were still hoping for a return by de Savary and the chance of some good copy over the ensuing months. On 2 May the *London Standard* stated: 'Peter de Savary has . . . declared his hand for the next America's Cup. Although his own attempt to mount a Challenge against the Australians failed at the eleventh hour, the millionaire businessman has thrown in his lot with another syndicate . . .'.

Meanwhile Tony Fairchild of *The Daily Telegraph* was cagily reporting the Royal Thames as saying they had interest from two groups, one with Cup experience, the other 'with support' from useful sources. He was also on hand to report the first denials of speculation about possible backers. 'We are not in a position to provide the £3m to £5m', said British Aerospace.

A post-deadline entry from the Japanese, accepted by the Royal Perth, received scant attention in Britain when the season of 'will we' 'won't we' began. By 7 May, just one week after the entry had been lodged, *The Daily Telegraph* prophetically announced: 'The British Challenge for the next America's Cup . . . is considered already to be seriously adrift in terms of development.' Two days later however, it offered the opinion that the 'second syndicate [is] thought to include yachtsman Robin Aisher and British Aerospace so the combination . . . could yet lead to a formidable British Challenge in Perth.'

Two more days and David Miller in *The Times* put us all out of our misery by disclosing that the Thames had plumped for the Easton approach, that West-Nally, the sports event brokers, were going to try and raise a maximum of £4.5m of sponsorship over the next six months, and added that 'a commercial airline offering reduced travel costs to Australia, will be added to the budget.' He also threw the name of Graham Walker into the arena, describing him as 'a retired Jersey businessman who was captain of last year's Admiral's Cup team', and Harry Cudmore 'an able but potentially provocative Sailing Manager'. Miller thought that the sail designer would be Angus Melrose, the helmsman would be Chris Law, and that Ian Howlett would be the designer. It was well predicted, though *Yachts and Yachting*

The radical glass-fibre 12 Metre Kiwi Magic, skippered by Chris Dickson, whose record in the Challenger Trials was near perfect.

Alan Bond's Australia IV — *worthy successor to the winged-keel 1983 Cup-winner* Australia II.

Two Kiwi 'Plastic Fantastics' duel before the trials. Kiwi Magic *was only the third 12 Metre ever to be built in glass-fibre.*

Tom Blackaller's USA, the most radical 12 Metre of the Cup series. Just visible from the air are her two rudders, fore and aft.

Chris Law steers White Crusader *in happier times before her elimination.*
Previous page Stars and Stripes, *skippered by Dennis Conner, was specifically designed for Fremantle's windy conditions.*

The New York Yacht Club's contender America II, *skippered by John Kolius, was eliminated before the Semi-Finals.*

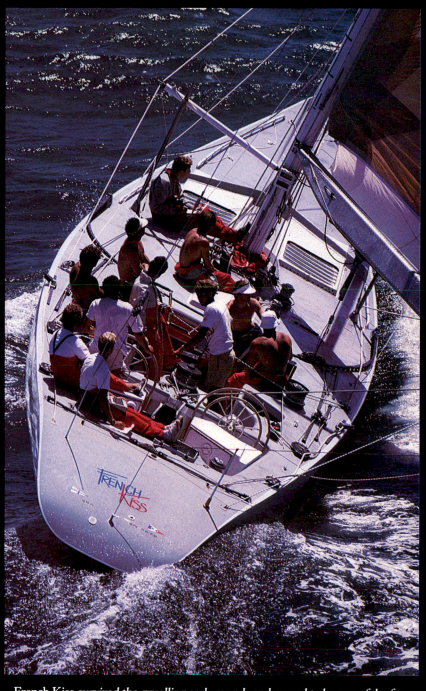

French Kiss *survived the gruelling early rounds and proved to be one of the four fastest 12 Metres of the series.*

Kevin Parry's Kookaburras *tuning together off Fremantle in late 1986. Video cameras in the masts read sail shape from the black bands.*

Kiwi Magic *was New Zealand's first-ever America's Cup Challenge. She pointed the way forward in glass-fibre construction techniques.*

with less flexible deadlines than *The Times* was still hedging its bets in June when Malcolm McKeag wrote:

Big question is who is to head the syndicate. For the life of it this column cannot see a better choice than the head it already appeared to have, but there is, or was, talk of inviting an established yachter to take the chair.

With the possible exception of Sir Maurice Laing – or perhaps Graham Walker – one cannot think of an established yachter to fit the bill. All likely candidates disqualify themselves by having too many of their own ideas on how to win and frankly the further Britain's yachting establishment is kept from this and any other challenge the better. You should expect Peter de Savary to be involved, but not deeply. He may not have known much about Twelves in 1980 but he does now and he still has half-a-million quids worth of kit to prove it. De Savary, with his special style of infectious dynamism will be to the effort what a tin of WD40 is to the owner of an ageing MGB: not the prime source of motive power but essential when all other remedies have failed. A quick squirt of de Savary will surely be needed to revive flagging spirits from time to time . . .

In the same magazine, same issue, John Chamier was saying, 'The British involvement at Fremantle is by no means cast iron and we, ourselves, will be surprised if it matures at all.' The *Southern Evening Echo* by mid-June had a confident headline saying 'AUSSIES WILL LOSE' and quoting Peter de Savary's opinion to prove it.

By the end of June *The Telegraph* was reporting that the Easton syndicate 'hopes to have a 12 Metre yacht sailing in Britain within a year' and possibly would take over the first *Victory*, later abandoned in favour of *Victory '83*, as a trial horse. The British were also beginning to play things long, 'we shall concentrate for the time [being] on an exhaustive research and development programme, for which we have excellent facilities for evaluation,' said the British syndicates lawyer Philip Tolhurst, 'testing theories is much cheaper than building boats'. By August *Seahorse* was pessimistic and sceptical, saying 'Whilst so much positive action is taking place around the world it is disappointing to see, or not to see as it appears, the lame British effort grinding to a halt.' After all there was still no established designer, according to *Yachting World* of the same month where the following correction appeared: 'Ian Howlett would like it known that, contrary to statements in our July issue, he has not made any arrangements to work with Admiral Easton's

America's Cup syndicate at this time.' Late September saw Sir Ian recruiting Phil Crebbin as Technical Director and claiming he was 'reasonably confident' of raising £4m but adding 'unless there was a high probability of success, with the money available at the start, there would be no point in continuing'. Indeed soon afterwards the *Guardian* reported that West-Nally were no longer involved, adding that the National Maritime Institute and David Hollom [?] were active on the design side. It was a flat report on the status quo – no judgements offered.

Not so the *Daily Mail*, which headlined a story on the 26 September 'OLD SEA DOG GETS HEAVE-HO' and said that Easton, who had no financial backing, 'is on the point of being scuppered'. With two years still to go before the elimination trials, things looked bad, although there was understandably no sense of urgency despite the fact that some syndicates were already sailing.

At last, in November, Easton announced that a team of sorts had been decided and responsibility for design was with David Hollom and Steven Wallis, working with Sir Herbert Pearcey at the National Maritime Institute. He was 'optimistic' about the £3.5m being raised. Meanwhile Southampton's *Southern Evening Echo* was indulging in its own brand of hype, telling its readers that President Reagan was reported to be heading one of nine American syndicates and followed this up by saying 'A brilliant winning design comes via inspiration and has nothing to do with brains, as it can occur to comparatively unknown designers.' Was this a veiled reference to Hollom?

1985 rolled in with a 2 January statement that £5.5m would be forthcoming and *The Times* saying: 'There were those who were muttering, following Admiral Easton's official announcement of the British Challenge on behalf of the Royal Thames Yacht Club on Wednesday, that the new campaign was beginning too late and with too little money. The evidence suggests this far from the case.'

IMP were now seeking sponsorship for Britain, and Graham Walker was emerging as the driving force. *The Guardian* was able to lead a story with the words 'A British Challenge for the America's Cup in 1987 is a virtual certainty.' Half the money had already been pledged but, while Sir Ian was the 'strategic genius', Walker was the man who had established the fund-raising structure for the company.

With no firm news it was left to *The Swindon Evening Adver-*

tiser to come up with the story. 'The designs of three boats which will take part in the race in Australia in 1987 are being kept under wraps until trials later this year', it said. There never were to be three boats as it transpired, but the Press at least responded warmly to both the management strengths and the line-up of top yachtsmen.

The year was off to a strong start. The widespread coverage was confident about the British Challenge and from Australia came news of hotel rooms being booked wholesale and budgets being so big that both the Italian and French Governments were involved.

The *Daily Mirror*, moreover, was pleased to announce that Sir Ian Easton, 'a distinguished man of the sea' had chosen a Mirror dinghy for his yachting pleasure. 'Now that's just the sort of information to make those Aussies sit up and take us seriously', it trumpeted with tongue firmly in its cheek. Actually the dinghy was for his son. He has a 25ft daysailer *Rona*.

At this time, too, although Ian Howlett was back in the camp and had been commissioned to design the first boat, all the attention was still on the Hollom work at the National Maritime Institute. The prospect of a breakthrough boat was allowed to capture the centre stage. In due course the contract for the first boat went to Whisstock's at Woodbridge, East Anglia, who were naturally delighted to have 'won in the face of strong competition from yards on the South Coast'.

That yard was in the midst of an expansion programme but its Marketing Director, Mr Anthony de Kerdrel, took time out to tell the *East Anglia Daily Times*, that, whilst *Australia II*'s winning secret had caused much controversy 'There will be no such ploys with the British Yachts.'

There was a little hiccough for the Thames' endeavours when *The Sunday Times* gratefully accepted from a journalist personally involved in the affair, a story guaranteed to steal their thunder at a crucial time. The Royal Torbay Yacht Club was putting together a Challenge for the 1990 event, had invited whizz-kidd Warwick Collins as a designer and top dinghy sailor Lawrie Smith as helmsman, and were after £20m. Much muttering and public banging of heads together by Ian Wooldridge in the *Daily Mail* saw things patched up – on the surface at least.

While orders for boats to be built in the future were made, and attention still focused on high hopes for the second, more radical design, the Thames forked out £163,500 for a site in Success Harbour for its America's Cup Headquarters, part of the Fremantle Sailing Club complex. Things were moving in the right direction again.

The scientific side, however, was still at the forefront of the British syndicate's propaganda strategy with the first boat expected to be at the 12 Metre World Championships in Australia in 1986.

Talking to the *West Australian* on 27 March, 1985 Sir Ian said: 'We're confident that Britain will undoubtedly produce one of the fastest and most technologically advanced 12 Metre boats in the world.' Still no money, though, until British Airways came to a kind of rescue in May when it offered £250,000 of flying time for people and gear making the long haul to Perth. So grateful was the syndicate that it painted the roof of its premises in BA colours and logo, and eventually had the boat used for publicity, flying a large spinnaker covered in the BA logo. The syndicate owed much to British Airways for that early support though they were never given centre stage.

First, though, they needed a boat. Whisstock's had gone into receivership and the search was on again for a yard that could take on the job. The size of that job, however, was in doubt as, by May, there was speculation that there would only be money enough for one boat. It was in May, too, that White Horse Whisky, then a trading brand of the Distillers Company, first announced their America's Cup connections. By agreement with the Royal Perth Yacht Club they would be the 'officially endorsed America's Cup brand for two years'. They paid £196,000 for the privilege.

The Thames overcame its reservations about continuing with the challenge when a group of members joined Graham Walker as underwriters of the project, but with an overall budget reduced to £3.5m. And East Anglia could briefly feel they may not have lost everything when Whisstock's went down. *The Telegraph* at the end of May said that Brooke Marine, also in Suffolk, was believed to be in line for the order. Encouragingly *The Times* told its readers on 28 May 'the syndicate is expected to name a major sponsor within the next few days'. Work was expected to start at Brooke Marine 'within the next two months'. *Yachting World* sort of agreed. 'Tate & Lyle are tipped as likely principal backers' they said.

By the end of July the British were engrossed in tank-testing and de Savary had sold his two Twelves, *Lionheart* and *Victory*, for, thought *The Telegraph*, 'a little more than £250,000'.

Into August, and the first inklings of the radical approach which Walker and his supporters were going to have to adopt to get over the problem of no cash. Writing in *The Times*, David Miller said 'Walker says a financial framework has been clearly established with the bankers and a comprehensive budget document for sponsors and sales promotion projects will soon be available'. Meanwhile the *Daily Mail* reported that the New York Yacht Club were 4–1 favourites to become the Challenger, Dennis Conner 5–1 and the Aga Khan's *Azzurra* 8–1. The British were not even mentioned.

Later that month, at long last, it was announced that the first British Twelve was under construction at Cougar Marine, Hamble, the site of the old Fairey Marine Yard. Fairey had built de Savary's second Twelve – *Victory '83* – and incidentally, Richard Branson's first *Virgin Atlantic Challenger*, which broke up so tantalisingly close to breaking the West–East transatlantic record.

Already the first boat would probably be too late for the important 12 Metre World Championships off Fremantle in February, 1986. But a hull was a serious intention and a second yacht was to be built immediately after the completion of the first. Just as important, less than two weeks later, the Diary column of *The Financial Times*, one of whose two daily compilers is an ardent yachtsman, announced the arrival of 'one of the most unusual documents' from the portentously named Guinness Mahon. 'Although a prospectus in style, it should rather be seen as a memorandum to potential punters,' it said rather starkly. 'And they will be reminded with brutal clarity that it is unlikely they will ever see their money again.' Even then, the Diary was talking in terms of patronage and sponsorship and when the syndicate announced on 18 September, 1985 that Princess Diana would perform the naming ceremony of the first boat, it was not until the sixth and final page of a long press release that they said, 'The syndicate has formed a Public Limited Company', and that a memorandum had been prepared.

Meanwhile new fund-raisers in the form of CSS promotions had been hired. They didn't last long either, but by now the Challenge's own momentum seemed to be picking up. The boat, as yet unnamed, would be ready for fund-raising duty at the London Boat Show of 1986.

With Chris Law, Jo Richards and Eddie Warden Owen joining the camp, Cudmore's role as first among equals was also looking like becoming a tough man-management problem. But at least the Torbay interlopers were now relegated to the inside pages of the *Western Morning News* as part of council deliberations on job creation.

The Press, meanwhile, was looking forward to their latest flirtation with Princess Di and the usual guessing game on the likely name was under way. Peterborough in *The Daily Telegraph* thought there were about 25 on the short list and included its own thought – *Pommie's Folly*. Just two days before the Princess swung the champagne bottle and lisped 'I name this ship *Crusader* . . .' the shock/horror of someone trying to sell the design secrets of the British yacht's keel to the New York Yacht Club hit the dailies.

So sportsmanlike had the New York Yacht Club become – or so unconcerned – that they sent the plans back, informed the British syndicate and the police, and helped set the trap which captured the alleged malefactor. John Anthony Brown, a worker at the Plymouth foundry where the keel would be cast, was questioned, released on bail, but in the end no charge was brought. It was the nearest so far to the skulduggery so beloved by America's Cup watchers.

On the eve of the christening ceremony in the cold and rather drab hangar-like building in which the Twelve, minus keel, was standing, *The Telegraph* dubbed the syndicate 'The scrimp and save Royal Thames'. Alan Bond, who was eventually to make his own £25,000 donation to the British attempt, excited as much yachting press attention as the boat itself, but while the Princess duly collared the lion's share of the editorial space, neither attracted as much coverage as the stolen secrets scandal. With the Boat Show looming, the British syndicate let it be known that the public would be able to buy shares in *Crusader* and the Challenge, though it is unlikely they thought that this would lead to a response of British Telecom proportions.

While the Brits went about the business of shaking their collection mugs, the Western Australia Government was doing its damnedest to encourage the tourism bonanza it was hoping for. They even brought over the 1983 Cup-winning helmsman, John Bertrand, to do his bit on the Boat Show stand.

As the man who had lifted the Cup, Dennis Conner's scalp, and Australian self-esteem to an all-time high, his views were eagerly sought. He wrongly foresaw that John Kolius who was to take over Conner's role for the New York Yacht Club would be in contention, and rightly that Conner himself, representing his San Diego Yacht Club, would be prominent. He told *The Times*: 'The British, I think, are potentially in a strong second category with the American *Eagle* syndicate and the Italians.' He was not far wrong in that either, as it happened.

Embarrassingly, the Brits couldn't raise the price of a charter for the World Championships, but as *Challenge France*, also suffering from budget difficulties, pulled out of that series in stepped a former Singapore-based English businessman, Ian Griffiths.

So, while the Royal Family managed to maintain the publicity impetus of the Challenge in the UK and the collection boxes rattled in Earls Court, Cudmore and Law with a crew of assorted Brits and Frogs prepared to have a crack at the Worlds. As for the Cup itself there were even some who, at that stage, were prepared to back their opinions with money. One of the big UK bookmakers, William Hill, reported 'unprecedented interest' in late January 1986. They were quoting the Americans as 4–6 odds-on favourites to win back the Cup and the Australians were rated 6–4 against to retain it.

Hardly anyone, including the visiting Bertrand, were bothering to mention the Kiwis except through odd references to the fact that they were raising a lot of money. William Hill, however, had had to reduce the odds against them rather rapidly from 14–1 when they took a bet of £2000 at that price. The New Zealanders, even at the end of January, could still be had for 6–1 as they joined Britain as joint third favourites.

Nearer to home and after all the disappointments for East Anglia, the *Ipswich Evening Star* came back valiantly to recharge morale when announcing, 'CUP YACHT TO GO VIA FELIXSTOWE'. Even to touch the hem, it seems, was important. Not half so important, though, as the little scheme dreamed up by accountants Stoy Hayward and promoted by the Bankers, Guinness Mahon.

Just seven weeks before the end of the financial year they invited investors to put up £3m using the provisions of a thing called 'the Business Expansion Scheme'. Under current British tax law, people paying tax at the top rate of 60 per cent of income could gamble on total relief of that tax if the money was invested for five years and could be realised at the end.

The *Daily Mail* at first thought the scheme would not come within the rules for tax exemption and Alice Rawsthorn in *The Financial Times* gave it a very deadpan write-up.

Richard Northedge in *The Daily Telegraph* was less coy. Describing it as 'possibly the most novel' of the BES propositions he said, 'This is possibly an investment for those prepared to lose much of their money, but who like sailing sufficiently to be able to boast in the clubhouse of how they played a small part in our America's Cup challenge.'

The *Daily Express* was less charitable. Under the headline 'STEER CLEAR OF THIS CHALLENGE', it said: 'We wish them luck in their sailing and in their fund raising. But we must state from the very beginning that this is no share issue for individual investors.

'Leaving aside the question as to whether this is the sort of project which should be funded, albeit indirectly, by the tax payer, it really is not a very sound investment.'

The Franglais team came 13th out of 14 in the 12 Metre Worlds, *New Zealand* was second to *Australia III*, and beat John Kolius in *America II*, and a certain 'Robert Fisher' writing in *The Financial Times* of 22 February said, 'The Kiwis could be a force to be reckoned with, particularly with a promise of a third, more radical boat to come.'

As a *Daily Mail*-inspired nationwide hunt for some winch-grinding strongmen unearthed two oarsmen capable of making the transition to sail power, David Arnold, a Director of British America's Cup Challenges, told *The Times* that the BES 'flotation' had been 'oversubscribed' and the £3m raised.

The crew followed the first boat to Australia and the Australian winter-long business of training and tuning began. Back home there was the inauspicious birth of the *Hippo*. No bands, no flags and no sponsors to name the result of all that concentration on British technology and the search for a breakthrough.

She was quietly shipped out; only a handful of reporters were present as she was towed down the Hamble. The following day the *Daily Mail* carried an exclusive report and photo by Adrian Morgan. *The Sunday Times* followed suit at the weekend. Everyone else, it seems, had been lured to London to attend a press conference, strategically timed to coincide with the launch of Britain's secret weapon.

Early reports from Fremantle were ecstatic about *Crusader*'s performance. Typical was a piece in the *Scarborough Evening News* of 16 May which said that not only had the British boat consistently '*in most conditions*' beaten *South Australia*, subsequently withdrawn during the trials, but was faster upwind and down than *New Zealand*.

'*Crusader*'s performance against *South Australia* is amazing,' said Harry Cudmore. '*Crusader* is right. She was right when she hit the water. Our tuning up has been confined to experimenting with sails and crew familiarisation. There hasn't been any need to alter the trim, much less make any major modifications. There are still other keels to try to improve our speed but there is no doubt we are going to be right in with the leaders.'

What a contrast to the frenzied activity of changing bow, keel, rudder and whole stern configuration that was to occur later between the second and third challenge Round Robins. With eyes now on the second boat and lots of encouraging noises being made there were also internal problems with one of the winners of the *Daily Mail* strongman competition – Mark Higgins – deciding that sailing was not for him. He left the British camp in Fremantle without even telling the management, to fly back to Birmingham where he had a business training night club bouncers.

Oh, and *Shoe and Leather News* were able to report that Dunlop Sports and Leisure Footwear would be helping to keep the British squad 'topside' during the competition because they had supplied them with their new Perth deck shoes.

As Perth is 12 miles from the action they were stretching the connection but not as much as the stretch from reality highlighted by Graham Walker in a July interview with Malcolm McKeag in *Yachts and Yachting*. 'Money is the thing that everyone focuses on. It is in fact the most boring aspect of it really,' a head-off that sat ill when, six months later, the syndicate was saying it had been beaten by money. He also said mid-way through: 'In the end it was the businessmen, not the yachtsmen, who made the Challenge possible.' Now we know whom to blame.

In the same edition of *Yachts and Yachting* David Arnold was telling Adrian Morgan that David Hollom's radical *Crusader 2* was good in both light winds and rougher conditions and Chris Law was adding, 'After the rudder change she now sails like a dream.'

The unlikely source of the *Daily Telegraph*'s Commercial

Correspondent, John Petty, brought further endorsement in early August. While the rest of the British yachting fraternity were winding up Cowes Week, he reported that Racal Electronics had contributed to the hi-tech security surrounding the British camp in Fremantle.

Turning to the second boat he quoted Harry Cudmore as saying, '*K25* is something special. She has the technological breakthrough needed to bring the cup home to Britain. We can't afford to give away the secrets of her revolutionary design.'

Other Challengers, said Petty, were 'scouring the air waves' to uncover the secrets in the British Challenger so 'secret signals' were being used, courtesy of Racal of course, to make sure that radio conversations on the performance of the *Hippo* could not be overheard.

The Times reported that, after moving the mast, the *Hippo* was faster upwind and down when the wind was either above 20 knots or below 10, and added that, at times she was 'dramatically faster than the Howlett design but then falls out of tune for no apparent reason'.

There were minor hiccoughs ashore, too. The Crusader Yacht Club, opened for investors and supporters at a reported cost of £200,000 was, according to the *London Standard*, seeking two chefs to fly out to Fremantle, much to the disgust of Aussies, who thought the jobs should be given to locals. The British Challenge director in the UK, David Arnold, said, 'I've been getting some ratty telexes saying "why don't you hire local girls rather than flying out English people?" But I think it's more sensible to have English staff. After all, I wouldn't want to run the risk of employing any spies while the races are going on.'

On 12 August in *The Times*, with less than two months to go before the first Round Robin of elimination trials began, David Miller was writing of a possible sponsorship deal involving a 'front-line multinational retail sponsor in Formula One Grand Prix racing'. Things were happening but in another direction.

Sister paper *The Sunday Times* took a look at spying between the rival syndicates saying at first it was rife and that Britain had spent £33,500, pretty exact that, to keep the keel secrets secret but ending with a quote from Technical Director Phil Crebbin saying: 'Snooping happened in the United States at Newport in 1983, but it's not going to affect us in Perth.'

In September's *Yachting World*, Tim Jeffery opened up a

lengthy feature by quoting Harold Cudmore as saying, 'I will offer no excuse if we lose. We have sufficient resources and sufficient opportunity. This is our chance.' It was now, also, that the back-pedalling on *Hippo* the Wonderboat began with Cudmore saying 'She's not a dog, but she's not going to stop the world.' And a strange Diary entry in *The Times* claimed that 'the British' – it didn't say which British – were taking advantage of the New York Yacht Club having set up credit accounts 'all over Perth'. The paper specifically quoted the example of a video rental shop where the use of passable American accents had meant that 'not only have the Americans coughed up the British hire fees, but paid the British fines as well'. Not our boys, surely!

Whether or not they were taking that opportunity, the Brits should have sat up and taken notice of Barry Pickthall's America's Cup diary of 21 August. With just six weeks to go, he consulted the bookmakers and wrote that the Americans were evens favourites to win back the cup and Australia 5–4 against to retain it.

Britain were third favourites at 5–1, Italy fourth at 8–1 with France and New Zealand equal fifth at 12–1. Oh for foresight the equal of hindsight.

Meanwhile in Fremantle Dennis Conner's *Stars and Stripes* goes aground while on tow to her dock. 'It's official', said the *West Australian* at the end of the month. Conner's wife Judy, in town for the duration with both daughters, was going to be a judge of the local radio station's competition to find the best recipe for a cocktail called 'Dennis on the Rocks'. The great man's reaction was not reported.

Getting stuck into less exotic, but more free-flowing cocktails, the announcement of the British Cup squad from among the 50 hopefuls led to a rather *too* enthusiastic dinner party at the Chez Orleans restaurant in Perth. Apparently the boys were throwing a few things around and disturbing other diners and so were asked to leave but, for once, the British Press let the matter drop pretty quickly. It was, said shore manager Spud Spedding, 'a storm in a teacup'.

Then came the financial breakthrough for the British Challenge. In the week of the Southampton Boat Show, where Harry Cudmore announced his crew, including the pairing of Chris Law at the helm and Eddie Warden Owen as navigator, Guinness stepped into the limelight.

To say that 1986 was a year under the spotlight for Guinness would be putting it mildly. They won an acrimonious battle with Argyll Foods for the control of the Distiller's Company, then took up the America's Cup Challenge and ended with an invasion of Department of Trade and Industry inspectors.

The White Horse Whisky company had already declared its intention to link closely with the America's Cup by becoming 'Official America's Cup Whisky'. They were also producing a calendar using Lord Lichfield as the photographer and a bevy of lovely leggy Australian models.

When Guinness next paraded chairman Ernie Saunders and UK Sports Minister Dick Tracey, it was to announce that up to £1.1 million would be provided in payments staged to reflect the level of success achieved by the British boat. The name of the Challenge would be changed to 'The White Horse Challenge' and the name of the boat would be *White Crusader*.

'Cheers', said the British Press, and there was a general feeling that Britain not only had the money, but had joined the club of those approved by big business. They were like the others now.

The America's Cup Ball in London, rounded off a bubbling week in which spirits were high and royalty back in attendance. It was summed up at the weekend in the *Observer* by Bob Fisher writing, 'Britain now has the best chance of winning the Cup since the schooner *America* took it from these shores in 1851.' Nor was the small irony missed that Graham Walker was a director of the Argyll Group which had fought so bitterly with Guinness.

Another less well publicised bitter battle was concluded in Australia when, at the end of September, it was announced that the more conventional *White Crusader* designed by Ian Howlett would be Britain's chosen campaign boat. 'We are choosing a boat which we believe will win,' said Harry Cudmore, though some wondered whether this was a bluff and that Cudmore would spring a switch ahead of the second Round Robin.

That decision, just one week ahead of the start of racing, was made public in the first of the weekly television programmes TVS was to bring to Channel 4 about the Cup competition.

So, with more than 30 boats from the various Defender and Challenger syndicates crowding the Fremantle waters, no less a man than Dennis Conner was telling the *International Herald Tribune* he thought the British entry would be in the final four. Britain had arrived.

And on the social side the Aussie Press was reporting that

royals would be flocking to the Fremantle dockside all around the world, that the *America II* syndicate was winning both wine-tasting and golf competitions and that a poll gave *Azzurra* the top spot as 'the crew most likely to enjoy themselves'.

For the most part, however, the competition was firmly locked onto the sports pages of the British Press with only minor forays into the area of general news. No-one tested public opinion on their knowledge or excitement about the America's Cup itself, or British chances, but if the opinion of the editors was anything to go by, they did not feel that the great British public was caught up in Cup Fever.

Never mind, at least Portsmouth could be told it was on the short list of venues to hold the 1990 America's Cup if Britain were to win in Fremantle. Sir Ian Easton, speaking to the *Portsmouth News* on behalf of the *Crusader* Challenge, said, 'If Britain wins the cup, and this is likely, then the defence in 1990 will be in September and tides, winds and sea room for courses appear to be acceptable in your area, which therefore means that it is on the short list.'

Attention was also centred on whether the glass-fibre New Zealand yacht was legal and whether there would be any problem for *White Crusader*'s change of name under the rules governing advertising and sponsorship.

That is, until the racing started. Britain began both well and ominously. In beating the radical *USA II*, skippered by Tom Blackaller, Cudmore and his crew had to come back from behind when repeated problems with the lock at the head of the mainsail saw the main tumble down to be hastily rehoisted. It was a tale of error to be repeated too often during the series.

At least the row over her name was thoroughly overshadowed by what was becoming known as the 'Glassgate affair'. Lloyd's Register of Shipping were stoutly defending their reputation and expertise, saying that their certificate of approval was good enough for the glass-fibre New Zealand yacht.

Conner, however, was leading the charge of suspicion, circulating all the other Challenge syndicates and asking them to support a move for new checks on hull construction by taking core samples.

The British won their name game, and New Zealand was eventually to survive the whole of the three Round Robins to meet Conner in the Challenger Finals though, despite Kiwi syndicate boss Michael Fay saying that test drilling of *KZ7*'s hull would be 'over my dead body', he gave way ahead of the Challenger Semi-Finals.

Plymouth entered the fray to host the 1990 America's Cup as the press indulged in not a little tittering behind cupped hands over a story that our flamboyant skipper Harry Cudmore had booted an innocent mainsheet trimmer and replied to the protest 'send it forward'.

Then Falmouth announced that it was in the running for the 1990 series as cash-register eyes lit up – even the *Yorkshire Evening Post* picked that up – the *Brighton Evening Argus* claimed an exclusive that the 1990 event may be coming there and *Crusader* finished the first series joint fourth with *USA II*.

Until now most attention had been on affairs at home with only the occasional report about activity by other syndicates such as Dennis Conner bashing himself, boats and crew through the waves off Hawaii. Conditions there were supposed to be the same as those to be expected when the big winds blew during the races off Fremantle.

But as soon as the racing began attention was finally focused on the town itself. As many people thought the event was taking place in Perth, which is 12 miles away, there was some readjustment to be made anyway. The town of Fremantle had been adjusting for some time to the promised invasion of the world's top yachtsmen, their camp followers, and the spectators.

The inevitable near-indignant revelation that rents were going up by a factor of ten were soon rife, with one syndicate boss being asked $300,000 a month for a very ordinary flat. It was profiteering on a grand scale. Ian Wooldridge, on 2 October in the *Daily Mail*, said a gold rush was on. He described Fremantle as Las Vegas-sur-Mer, with yachts to charter at £1m-plus and the Indian Ocean for sale in bottles at £16; £23 for magnums.

In mid-December, Ivor Davies in the *Daily Express* told his readers, 'Fremantle, once the sleepy, down-on-its-luck port town for Perth, is now on the jet set's "must" list. "Old Free" is right up there with Monte Carlo, Gstaad, Sardinia and Rio.'

The Aussies must have loved that. Though they would not have been so happy about a book review in *The Daily Telegraph* by Tony Fairchild on *How to Survive in Australia*. 'You can say anything as long as it's not backed up with facts,' he quoted, adding that the book never even mentioned yachting, yachtsmen, or the America's Cup and that the Aussies' number one sportsman was the golfer Greg Norman.

Mostly the attention was on events on the water, with the twin shoreside distractions of the legality, or otherwise, of the New Zealanders' glass-fibre boat, and the attempts by the Brits to have a keel cast in Australia, rather than make it in Plymouth and airfreight it out.

Even as *White Crusader* went into battle, Bob Fisher reminded us in *The Guardian*, on 29 September that there could be some deception in the choice of the more conventional Ian Howlett boat. 'The real point of the choice is probably to fool the opposition', he said. 'At this stage there is more than meets the eye to various boats and Cudmore is the biggest tongue-in-cheek man in Fremantle.

'He will be giving both boats a full chance of providing him with a winner and the trials between the two boats in the British camp are to continue. The Hollom design is far from being written off.'

As part of the more conventional hype, pipe bands and supporters' parties were all the rage, apparently, and it was *International Freighting Weekly*, in October, with picture, that said that syndicate boss Graham Walker's 1933 open Rolls-Royce Phantom was being shipped to Fremantle where it was 'intended as a runabout for the White Horse Challenge Team'. Wow!

Other light relief came in the form of a big piece in *The Times* describing how the British camp had tried and failed to train a rat called 'Crebs' (Phil Crebbin was the Technical Director) to run the length of the mast with a piece of line usually, paradoxically called a mouse, which could later be used to pull through halyards or wire. 'Crebs', we were told, had a habit of curling up and going to sleep half-way.

We were also told that, in contrast to Walker's preference for all that is best in British cars for himself, he had banned the more modern variety from the White Horse dock because the industry in the UK had not sufficiently supported him.

The Financial Times, in more cultural vein, noted that Tim Thompson, an artist from Cornwall, had been commissioned to paint every one of the 26 Defence and Challenge contenders, with *The Telegraph* adding that the Brits were having a bash at the supporters' club with Jimmy Edwards and Ronnie Corbett at centre stage. Well, there's style.

On more serious matters, and away from men being washed

overboard or the writing of the obituary for *Courageous*, *The Telegraph* also said, at the end of Round Robin 1 'of all the dark horses galloping towards the America's Cup in 1987 *New Zealand* is surely the darkest'. And with a very prescient piece on 29 October, followed this up by saying that Tom Blackaller's *USA II* would be the biggest threat to *White Crusader*'s progress and was the favourite to produce the biggest improvement. And how.

On the second day of Round Robin 2 Blackaller was beating Conner, having lost in the first round, and on the third day the Brits were doing their own bit for the edge-of-the-seat enthusiasts by beating *Canada II* with a margin of 0.328 of a second. Unfortunately they went out the next day against John Kolius of the New York Yacht Club and had grinder Paul Rushent in hospital after being pinned against a winch drum by a genoa sheet, bent a spinnaker pole, and had to cut away a spinnaker washed overboard. 'Unfortunate', said Harry.

Next day the mast went as either a running backstay block pin failed or someone failed to pin the running backstay and the next day a genoa sheet parted during the final beat against *New Zealand*.

Then we beat Conner and the mood was suddenly euphoric, we beat *Eagle* and moved into third place, and then *French Kiss* burst the bubble as a genoa was blown, Mel Coleman went overboard, and we finished the series in fifth place.

Conner himself was still grumbling about the legality of New Zealand's boat and the British camp was still fighting to have a keel cast in Australia as *White Crusader* came in for some major surgery to the bow, stern, rudder and keel.

The story of that final Round Robin was one of protests, desperately near misses, more gear failure, changes at the last minute in the composition of the afterguard as Eddie Warden Owen was replaced by Phil Crebbin and the exit.

There was a little flurry between the *Daily Express*, saying that Princess Anne was tempted to cancel official engagements on a visit to Perth because Princess Michael would be there as a guest of Peter de Savary 'who is backing the British entry', and the *Daily Mail*. The *Mail* took great pleasure in debunking the story.

There was also some disagreement between the *Daily Express* writers on how the round-up of the British story should be handled. On 15 December they said that the British Challenge had been blown away but ... 'this time, at least, there was no disgrace'. On 16 December they published 'the team should assess the damage done to British sailing by this latest failure ... worst of all the effect that yet another cup failure will have on the sport in Britain'.

Most scathing was Wooldridge in the *Mail*. The best that could be said was that nobody drowned, he wrote. After that it was a 'disaster'. Was the entire campaign foiled by 'self-deception'?

The Press, true to form, had gone full circle – from amusement through scepticism to euphoria and condemnation. It was ever thus. . . .

CHAPTER SEVEN
The Kiwi Dark Horses
Chris Freer/Adrian Morgan

The plans of New Zealand's three glass-fibre 12 Metres are kept in a grey, locked filing cabinet at Lloyd's Register of Shipping's offices in Southampton. Even in late 1986, long before the final outcome, the surveyor in charge of their construction had predicted remarkable things: 'We have seen the birth of a new generation of 12 Metres. I can foresee the day when aluminium is obsolete.'

By the time *Kiwi Magic* met Dennis Conner's *Stars & Stripes* in the best-of-seven Challenger Finals, she was set for her fiercest test to date. In her 38 previous races the Kiwi boat had beaten all the other Challengers save Conner himself. By the start of the first race of the Finals the tally was 2–1 to the Kiwis. The myth of Kiwi invincibility was to take a lot of knocks by the time the gunsmoke-blue *Stars & Stripes* had earned the right to meet the Australian Defender, *Kookaburra III*.

The Kiwis' innovative yacht was not the first in the history of the Cup to frighten those without the knowledge or nerve to try something a little bit different.

Ever since the schooner *America*, that 'sparrow-hawk among pigeons', trounced the British fleet in 1851, fear of the unknown has been a powerful weapon in the process of winning the America's Cup. Long before she appeared over the western horizon ripples of apprehension had crossed the Atlantic.

Fear of the unknown again played its part in *Australia II*'s victory in 1983. By the time the 'little white pointer' met *Liberty*, her near invincibility had become an article of faith. In 1986 it happened yet again. The performance of *Kiwi Magic* (*KZ7*) in the America's Cup Trials, winning 37 out of 38 races, was little

82

short of miraculous – a view which the Kiwis were slow to refute and quick to foster. Fear of the unknown again stalked the streets of Fremantle.

Kiwi Magic was fast, but how much of her speed was due to her unique glass-fibre construction and how much to her hull shape, sails and crew work was a matter of fierce debate.

That *Kiwi Magic*'s design was good was never doubted. The sailing fraternity have long recognised the talents of her sailors and designers, in particular Laurie Davidson, Ron Holland and Bruce Farr, and the remarkable 25-year-old helmsman, Chris Dickson. For a small country to have so much sailing talent is one of the remarkable facts of the yachting world.

It was therefore no surprise that the 1986 Challenge, the Kiwis' first ever, turned out to be strong. Who can forget 1967 when Chris Bouzaid and his little yacht *Rainbow* came from the land of long white cloud to win every race in sacred Cowes and then run on to take the World One Ton Cup. The New Zealanders have always been world class.

The Kiwis got off to a strange start when, only a few days before the deadline for lodging Challenges, Martin Fascher, a Belgian entrepreneur resident in Sydney, put up the $AUS16,000 deposit. Fascher, together with Don Brook, a leading figure in the Royal New Zealand Yacht Squadron, only had time to create a basic project plan before they hit trouble with funding and bowed out. His disappearance, almost as sudden and mysterious as his arrival, left a vacuum soon to be filled by new, but well-qualified, alternatives.

It is debatable whether the merchant bankers Fay and Richwhite fully realised the true import of their actions when they took over the campaign back in 1984. The Perth version of the America's Cup had yet to be recognised as the event that would change yachting from a minority interest sport to one of public appeal. Nevertheless there can be no doubt that the decisions made in the early part of the management process were far reaching and demonstrated a very mature approach to a seemingly impossible task.

Two important factors were to initiate the successes of the syndicate; first was the decision to build two identical boats as trial horses; the second was to build them using the recently legalised glass reinforced plastic technique (glass-fibre or GRP). The latter route posed big problems because the construction rules were couched in such a way as to have proved insurmountable by other seemingly better qualified syndicates.

The approach to the design work was also enlightened and in the same way that it took nearly 50 years for us to discover the true designer of *Ranger*, the revolutionary J Class yacht which won the Cup in 1937, so it may be with the Kiwi series of hulls. The combined knowledge of Holland, Farr and Davidson, with their extensive resources and campaign experience, gave the project credibility from the start. An early decision also gave each designer equal credit for the success. The fact remains that for a first shot at the difficult 12 Metre Class Rule, the boats were extraordinarily free from problems, and were on the pace from the beginning, especially when compared to the painful development processes of Dennis Conner and his experienced team in the *Stars & Stripes* camp.

Construction of two identical boats at Marten Marine and McMullen & Wing gave the team the facility of using one as a bench-mark with the second yacht acting as a development test bed. Using this approach permitted full-scale testing of fundamental, as well as radical, features of design or sailing techniques.

Working from a known reference point of performance has always been the best method of obtaining rapid, valid results. The British tried to develop two different yachts and failed, and it is significant that the *Kookaburra* syndicate worked in the same way as the Kiwi team and were successful. With hull design showing only refinements once the basic decision of displacement had been made, the most important design factor for the Perth series remained the keel. The importance of this has already been described in the tale of Peter Cole and his *Steak 'n' Kidney* design where the wrong choice of keel resulted in early defeats from which the boat would never recover, even when the correct keel eventually transformed her performance.

The New Zealanders' main tank work on hull and keel design was carried out at the relatively small tank of the Wolfson Unit in Southampton, England. Initial approaches to the NSMB run by Peter Van Oossanen, the keel guru who supervised Ben Lexcen's experiments on *Australia II*, were abandoned in favour of an outfit that seemed to offer better value as well as an enthusiastic and professional approach. Although the Americans regarded the NSMB as ahead in the vital area of keel design correlated to actual boat performance, the Wolfson Unit offered low-speed wind tunnel research facilities as well as hull/keel computer performance prediction, all ably managed by Andy Claughton, a veteran tankman on 12 Metres. Moreover their security was absolute, a necessary factor due to their test programme on the British boats, which was taking place at the same time.

In their search for performance gains the New Zealand design team constantly tested models of their competitors keels, whether the ideas seemed crazy or not. It transpired that of all the weird devices seen under the Twelves in Perth only *USA*, with her radical bow rudder configuration, proved capable of competing on level terms with the 'conventional' winged-keel refinements. The Kiwis' final solution incorporated a modest bulb to get the weight low, and relatively conservative wings.

The problems Tom Blackaller encountered in his development of the Gary Mull designed *USA* are now well known. The control machinery had to be very complex to balance the forces acting on the boat in a seaway correctly and yet allow her to sail consistently fast. Canard jet fighters using similar geometry can only fly under computer control because the pilots cannot react or manipulate the lifting surfaces accurately or quickly enough. *USA* had similar problems with the high-aspect, heavily-loaded, quick-stalling foils at each end of the hull. The bow rudder had to turn through high angles to achieve manoeuvrability on the start line and yet be controlled incrementally up the windward beat. The helmsman, Blackaller, steered in the conventional way with the stern rudder while a second man wrestled with the problem of balance by matching the bow rudder angle to computer data which offered a solution to the constantly varying loads of racing. Setting the boat up during and after a tack in a seaway involved considerable juggling and probably indicates why *USA* avoided tacking duels wherever possible.

Although glass-fibre construction offered a quick turn-round in terms of hull construction, cracking the problem of making a legal boat was not easy. Lloyd's Register of Shipping lay down rules for the construction of 12 Metres in wood, aluminium and latterly glass-fibre. Regardless of which system is chosen the hull weight and the distribution of that weight should be the same. The fact remains that wood absorbs water and is also structurally less stiff than aluminium which in turn is heavier for a given strength and stiffness than glass-fibre built under controlled conditions. Lloyd's were canny and left it to the designers to offer equivalent glass-fibre construction solutions and then made the task nearly impossible by insisting on what could be construed as some old-fashioned moulding methods. The experience of the Kiwi design team was the vital ingredient. All of the designers in the syndicate had made the change from aluminium to advanced composite structures in their ocean racers years before. They felt that glass-fibre was the material to go for if only they could use it to its correct advantage.

Although the New Zealand designers were convinced from the outset, other designers flatly refused to acknowledge the superiority of the Kiwis' chosen material. The first argument was that *KZ7* was no breakthrough; there was no way that a glass-fibre boat could be superior to an aluminium boat built according to Lloyd's rules. Holland, Farr and Davidson had done their job well. The rest was due to superb sailing by the Kiwi skipper, Chris Dickson, and his crew.

It's an argument that had been applied to *Australia II* four years earlier, not least by her skipper, John Bertrand. Certainly the winged keel gave her an edge in certain conditions, but sails, crewing and the fear she engendered in her opponents were equally important. Any one of these could have given her the vital edge. There was no magic involved.

The second commonly held view was that *KZ7* was fast because the Kiwis somehow managed to pull the wool over Lloyd's eyes and incorporated banned material in her construction. It was a view held by Dennis Conner, who was keen to drill holes in her to see if he could find little incriminating strands of carbon fibre or Kevlar, banned by Lloyd's rules. Most of those, like Marc Pajot's *French Kiss*, who had met *KZ7* and come away bloody-nosed in the Semi-Finals could only pray that this was indeed the case. It was a futile hope.

The third option was that the Kiwis, without in any way deluding Lloyd's, had managed to find a way to build a breakthrough boat in relatively sophisticated, but low-tech, glass-fibre – R and S glass and Nomex core material – with perhaps an aluminium space frame to take the loads, but without exotica, thus complying fully with the rules.

These state: 'GRP yachts shall not be of less weight, nor have a more beneficial weight distribution nor be less strong than an aluminium yacht built strictly in accordance with the requirements laid down in the design study carried out by Lloyd's Register of Shipping for aluminium yachts (Dated June 1971).

(IYRU Keel Boat Committee, 1982 Yearbook page 119.) Less strong shall mean both strength and stiffness.'

Simply stated, the Kiwis, quite legitimately and in full view of Lloyd's, built a yacht which met Lloyd's criteria, was stiffer fore and aft and thus potentially faster, yet little or no heavier than an aluminium yacht.

The first of these views was held by Ian Howlett, the British designer of *Lionheart*, *Victory '83* and *White Crusader*. He categorically denies that glass-fibre has any advantages over aluminium in the construction of 12 Metres according to Lloyd's rules. There is no way that the materials they allow would produce a stiffer yacht. He attributed the Kiwis' early speed quite simply to pure yachting ability. The rest was hype. In any case a marginal increase in stiffness fore and aft, even if it were possible, would be minimal in terms of deflection. 'Designers can only do a certain amount. There's no substitute for yachting it right.'

Howlett went down the glass-fibre path in 1983 and found a blind alley. 'We explored glass for *Victory* in 1982', he said. 'Lloyd's told us that they would make sure it came out 12 per cent heavier to ensure there was no advantage. If there was any advantage in GRP, and if it's stiffness and strength we want then why don't we build masts out of it?', he added succinctly.

Howlett believes that Lloyd's were so anxious to avoid what happened when aluminium replaced wood, when it was suddenly possible to build up to 3000 lb. lighter, that they stacked the odds against the new material to deter designers.

The second rather alarming opinion, that the Kiwis had used banned materials, was too fanciful to entertain, and by the end of 1986 there were core samples from the boat to prove it. In any case, to have deluded Lloyd's would have been virtually impossible given the level of scrutiny. To delude the world would have been to risk appalling consequences in the white heat of America's Cup scrutiny.

The process of design approval involved not only checking the weight calculations submitted by the designers, but also physically weighing every ounce of fibre and resin that went into the boat. Normally the Lloyd's surveyor is called in only at crucial stages in the construction of an alloy 12 Metre. In the case of the Kiwi 12 Metres he was there all the time, an operation that was said to have cost at least £50,000. It was an expensive gamble. The truth seems to be that where others failed to persevere, the Kiwi syndicate, with their knowledge of advanced glass-fibre techniques prevailed and gained the advantage of a yacht hull about 30 per cent stiffer than the opposition and five per cent lighter. In real terms this meant that the massive rig forces in the modern boats were resisted without the rigging and mast flexing as much as the competition. This allowed the sails to work better by transmitting power more directly. The advantage was greater in the higher wind strengths and heavy inertial wave conditions encountered in Perth. Racing cars gain in a virtually identical way when a chassis can be made stiffer and lighter. The idea is not new.

The Lloyd's surveyor, Jamie Course, also agreed that the Kiwi 12 Metres were stiffer than their rivals, perhaps by as much as 20 per cent. He was not surprised, therefore, that *KZ7* was fast. 'We have no jurisdiction over sailing ability', he said. 'Stiffness is allowed under the rules and is a factor in the performance of a sailing boat. If you can load the forestay up you get a better set and we know that the Kiwi 12 Metres are carrying an awful lot of mast compression.'

Slight modifications to the overall form of the Kiwi yachts were made for the third and final hull. All three boats were, however, made on the same male mould in New Zealand. All were supervised night and day. The early carping from Dennis Conner was proved to be groundless gamesmanship. The Kiwis did not spend $10 million to be caught cheating. They knew they had a legal advantage in this vital area.

Course is quite certain that nothing was left to chance:

All the boats were fully within the requirements. If anything, I think that the GRP boats are more legal than any other 12 Metre ever built. Firstly the surveyor is around all the time and secondly, unlike aluminium hulls where there is no way of telling if a plane or sander has been used, in GRP you can see very easily any attempts at sanding or filling.

We are talking of very high tolerances and very small differences. Every piece was weighed before it went in; all tools; all materials in the vacuum process to allow for pick-up of resin. We are talking about a degree of weight control far in excess of any GRP marine construction ever built before.

We were more than 100 per cent satisfied that the requirements were fulfilled. The sandwich or single skin had to be constant with no 'taper' as it were, i.e. the laminate was uniform throughout the length of the yacht with no 'lightened' ends.

Apart from the construction and the dedicated development programme there was one other feature of the boats which played a significant part. The Kiwi yachts were the widest boats by over a foot. The extra beam can be seen on photos and was applied in the area of the sheet tracks, well aft. This allowed the sheeting angle of the genoas to be eased outboard by as much as four degrees in heavy weather, opening the slot or gap with the mainsail. This also allowed much more efficient sail setting as well as reducing the heeling forces in strong winds. Although pointing ability can be affected by doing so, the boat speed is usually increased. The idea for doing this lay with the experience of the design team, two of whom, Bruce Farr and Laurie Davidson, were the pioneers of fractional-rig IOR racing yachts. They must have found the traditionally narrow 12 Metre deck platform very restrictive on first acquaintance.

Because of the way the campaign funding was organised the Challenge never lost momentum due to financial constraints, and while Dennis Conner's progress towards the Finals had been methodical, the Kiwis' had been meteoric. Under her young skipper, Chris Dickson, the Kiwi yacht had achieved something which no country had ever achieved before. Despite being the smallest in the Cup, New Zealand, a country of some three million people had put together a Challenge that looked set to make the grade at its first attempt.

As news of Dickson's continuing successes filtered back to those at home, excitement reached fever pitch. The fundraising committee backed by the Bank of New Zealand harnessed the enthusiasm of the Kiwis to an extent never before seen in any sport. Local DJs would preface their programmmes: 'Doesn't it make you want to sing, to be a part of God's own?'. Keith Harper, in *The Guardian*, reported: 'Most towns are now ablaze with floral displays celebrating the success of *KZ7*'. Prices of seafront property in Auckland began to rise. Victory Bonds were on sale at banks at above-average interest rates. At every new triumph the stock market jumped a point. 'The Cup message has been taken the length and breadth of New Zealand', wrote Harper. In a grand gesture, New Zealand's Premier, David Lange, offered himself as reserve crewman, if it would help. A pop song called *Sailing Away*, to the tune of a Maori love song, was top of the charts. At the height of the final battle with Dennis Conner's *Stars & Stripes*, a thousand messages of support were flooding into the fax machines at the Kiwi headquarters. After one race Dickson said: 'It was worth a tenth of a knot to us'.

As *Kiwi Magic* set out for the race course each day she was cheered on her way by thousands of Kiwi supporters, including a Maori war party evoking the gods of the winds and waves to the cause.

Conner won the first race by one minute 20 seconds. Anyone who thought that Dickson would crack under the pressure was proved utterly mistaken. Dickson, whose steely blue eyes had earned him the nickname 'The U-Boat Commander', drove his glass-fibre yacht with a confidence and maturity that surprised even Dennis Conner with 10,000 sailing hours in 12 Metres under his substantial belt.

Kiwi Magic, however, soon proved to have an Achilles' heel. Upwind the powerful boat from San Diego gained relentless on the bird-like *KZ7*. It was the start of a pattern that would repeat itself over the next few days. Dickson would match Conner in pre-start manoeuvres, only to lose on the drag race to the top mark. Conner likened *Stars & Stripes* to a 'top fuel dragster'. *Kiwi Magic* was like a turbocharged Porsche – fast round the corners but no match on the straight.

Day two saw Conner finishing ahead once again. 'We know that fifth gear exists in our Porsche, but we're having a little bit of a problem getting into it out there in the chop', said Dickson after his second defeat. The Kiwis' only hope seemed to lie in engaging Conner in a tacking duel, where they could dictate terms. Their chance came in the third race; 21 seconds down at the first mark, Dickson pounced on *Stars & Stripes* when a clip attaching her spinnaker to its halyard failed on the downwind leg. As the *Stars & Stripes* crew dragged the sodden sail aboard, Dickson drove *Kiwi Magic* to within a boatlength, forcing Conner to engage in a series of desperate gybes that left the New Zealanders out in front at the bottom mark by six seconds.

Although Conner's sail was up and pulling again within four minutes, the Kiwis were now ahead. Once on the hook Dickson matched Conner tack for tack in an exhausting duel – 128 tacks later Conner was still behind. It was a classic match race, the margin between the boats never more than half a minute. On the final, brutal beat to windward Conner tacked 55 times in the three and a quarter mile leg. *Kiwi Magic* crossed the line 38 seconds ahead.

The next day's racing was a disaster. With the wind gusting to 30 knots again, Gage Roads was a mass of white-flecked water. A desperate crash gybe ripped the Kiwis' backstay out, destroying their masthead instruments. Dickson and his crew were fortunate to finish at all as, close to the line, their mainsail disintegrated into ribbons. With the series now 3–1 to Conner the Kiwis called a lay day to nurse their wounds and replace their damaged mast.

19 January saw *Kiwi Magic* in a near hopeless position, but nowhere near ready to throw in the towel. *Star & Stripes* again dominated the first upwind leg, powering into a big lead at the top mark. Although the result was predictable, the race was not. As gale force winds drove vicious white caps across the race course, the contest turned into a close, often dangerous, trial between the two very dissimilar yachts.

If Dickson was on the ropes at the top mark, he never showed it. Downwind *Kiwi Magic* took 19 seconds off *Stars & Stripes*, surfing to within a few boatlengths. Upwind, however, it was the same story as before until Conner's headsail exploded under the strain. As the crew dragged it down, ditching it finally into the sea, *Kiwi Magic* closed to 14 seconds at the mark and, setting a brand new genniker – a cross between a spinnaker and a genoa – she again showed devastating offwind speed, reducing the margin to just eight seconds at the wing mark. A poor sail change allowed Conner to slip away yet again, and by the next windward mark he was 36 seconds ahead.

Dickson again attacked downwind, driving *KZ7* to within striking distance. Close to the last mark it seem as if the Kiwi yacht would roll over *Stars & Stripes* and take the lead. It was not to be. In the heat of the battle Dickson clipped the orange course buoy, and by the time *Kiwi Magic* had rerounded it, Conner was gone. It was an extraordinary end to the New Zealanders' hopes. In three hours of racing they had fought back to within boatlengths of the veteran American crew, only to fail at the very last hurdle.

In the end it was Dickson who summed it up best when he said at an emotional press conference: '13 years' beat 13 months' experience'. But in those 13 months the Kiwis had come closer to the America's Cup than anyone ever dared to predict. *Kiwi Magic*'s record of 38 wins in 43 races will stand as an incredible epitaph for a Challenge that brought together a nation and took it to within a hair's breadth of yachting's Holy Grail.

CHAPTER EIGHT

First Defence, Last Laugh

Adrian Morgan

By the time Tony Liversuch, proprietor of Crazy Charlie's in Queen Victoria Street, Fremantle, considered repainting the sign above his shop to KOOKA FOR THE CUP, the writing had been on the wall of the Bond syndicate camp for some weeks. For months prior to *Kookaburra III*'s 5–0 victory over Alan Bond's *Australia IV* the sign had read BONDY FOR THE CUP. At least someone in Fremantle was not slow to acknowledge the victors. Once Australia followed his example the *Kookaburra*'s laugh took on a less abrasive and altogether more popular note.

As soon as it became obvious that the Parry and Bond syndicates' yachts would be fighting out the Defender Finals, their personalities, and squabbles became the focus of media interest in the Defence efforts. Although Bond eventually lost the contest on the water there is no doubt that he convincingly won the public relations war that had raged from the moment the one-time Perth sign-painter discovered that the furniture maker's son had joined the exclusive Royal Perth Yacht Club and intended to have a crack at Bond's own attempts to defend the Cup he had spent 12 years winning.

Bond's Boxing Kangaroo had taken on the status of an alternative national flag following *Australia II*'s Newport victory, and his 1983 battle hymn, Men at Work's *I come from a Land Down Under* another national anthem. United under them, Australia's first Defence became synonymous with Bond, and his flag its symbol. Against such strong emblems, Parry's laughing *Kookaburras* stood little chance. His attempts at winning the support of Australia seemed to take second place to his dedication to organising the best possible Defence campaign. By the middle of January the *Kookaburras* may have been going fast, but Parry's public image was sinking even more rapidly.

If there was nothing to say, Parry would remain silent. If there was, either he or skipper Iain Murray would present facts and fend off queries. It seemed that they were impatient to get on with the job, and only grudgingly paid lip service to public interest. Where the Taskforce could so easily have played on their rôle as underdogs – the new kids in town up against the bully boys on the block – they ended up looking like upstarts, and aggressive ones at that. The *Kookaburras* were not the most popular of birds.

Bond's campaign could not have been handled more differently; he had learnt what public support could do both in victory and defeat and used this knowledge brilliantly. From his stumbling, foot-in-mouth efforts of Newport in 1977, Bond had developed into a lovable, round-faced rascal, a true son of his adopted country, a champion of the America's Cup faith, and a man who, despite his continuous eye on the main chance, had not just his own, but Australia's, interests at heart. In the capable hands of Bond's operations supremo Warren Jones, the genial tycoon's handling of both press and public was masterful. In 1983 Jones had masterminded the Australian counter-attack to the New York Yacht Club's allegations; in 1986/87 his role was to make sure that the late-starting *Kookaburras* did not get the last laugh.

Although both Bond and Parry were predicting that their corporations would be between $AUS 5 and 7 million in the red as a direct result of the Cup Defence, there is little doubt that Bond's was the better investment in commercial terms.

If it had been unthinkable in 1983 that Alan Bond would win the trophy from the Americans, it was doubly so that he would not be defending it in 1987. Although *Australia IV*, Ben Lexcen's latest creation, had been slow off the starting blocks in the long preliminary rounds, by mid January she was a nose in front of her nearest rival, Kevin Parry's *Kookaburra III*, and firm favourite to meet Dennis Conner's *Stars & Stripes*, or *Kiwi Magic* on 31 January.

Kookaburra III's swoop into the Defender's berth was as much of a surprise to the Bond syndicate as it was to the Australian people, many of whom were still under the impression that Bondy automatically held the right to defend the Cup. Some even thought he owned it. He did not. In 1983 he won it for his home club, the Royal Perth. One could be forgiven for believing that Bond, its most famous member, not only owned the Cup but also the Club. At times it seemed that he owned Australia too. While the battle for the Defence was taking place, Bond's pugnacious profile was seldom out of the news; while the Bond airship, emblazoned with his Swan Lager logo, flew above the waters of Gage Roads, closer to earth the contest between Bond's brewery and Taskforce sponsor Fosters threatened to turn the contest into a battle of the breweries – Lager Wars. Parry and Bond fought each other on every prime-site billboard the length of the land.

Of the four syndicates that lined up for the Defence, only two: Parry's Taskforce '87 and Bond's Defence had any realistic chance of surviving through to the Finals. Bond's first yacht *Australia III*, developed by Bex Lexcen from the 1983 Cup winner, was soon showing her famous elder sister the way home in all but the lightest weather. Built for the big seas off Fremantle, *Australia III* proved herself early on by beating the world's best Twelves in the World Championships in 1986, a regatta from which the Taskforce was conspicuously absent.

Although Bond was the first to point out the danger of predicting an America's Cup match racing victory from the results of a fleet race, the syndicate were at least confident that they were on the pace, though they had no way of judging the performance of the *Kookaburras*. As the series progressed the new yachts began to edge away from their rivals. The Bond/Parry millions were more than a match for the less well-heeled competitors from the south and east.

With the South Australia syndicate's 12 Metre eliminated early in the Trials and the Sydney yacht *Steak 'n' Kidney* embarrassingly slow (although she did show blistering speed once the unfortunate mix-up with her keels had been rectified), the stage was set for a showdown between Perth's rival millionaires.

Although the Parry syndicate had been slow off the mark, they were not short on experience. In 28-year-old Sydneysider Iain Murray they found a man with the mentality to take a slow-starting campaign by the scruff of the neck and make up for lost time. By August 1986 the Taskforce syndicate had launched, trialled and evaluated three 12 Metres. If Bond, who had rejected an early advance by Murray to join his camp, was not publicly showing his concern, many felt he should have been.

What was emerging, however, was a growing antagonism between the Man who Won the Cup and the man who seemed determined to rob him of the chance to defend it. Both on and off the water the two rival syndicates spared no opportunity to play the rules to the last comma. By the end of the Defender Trials, there had been no fewer than 50 protests in just over 100 races between the white-hulled *Australias* and the golden *Kookaburras*, and a war of words that reminded one of the worst days of 1983. While Bond played the sarcastic bully to Parry's bluntness under the television lights, their skippers; Murray, Gilmour, Beashel and Lucas barged, pushed and protested at sea. With Bond's decision to sideline the flagging *Australia III* and concentrate on *Australia IV*, the Parry syndicate was emerging as a force to be reckoned with.

The rivalry between the two syndicates was the inevitable reflection of the big business interests that were involved in the Defence effort. The war of words reached its climax just prior to the final selection Trials in January. Warren Jones called the *Kookaburra* crew 'dingoes' – afraid to fight on the water, they were relying on protests, he claimed. When *Australia IV* unfurled a new secret genniker sail, a cross between a spinnaker and a genoa, and proceeded to win a vital race, *Kookaburra III*'s red flag was flying almost immediately. If *Kookaburra III* won the protest and *Australia IV* lost, the Royal Perth were faced with the prospect of a one syndicate, two-boat play-off for the Finals. Bond's boat being eliminated on a technicality would have provoked an outcry. The *Kookaburras* were hauled in front of the committee and given a sharp lecture. A face-saving deal was reached between the two syndicates, but was in the event unnecessary. *Australia IV* won her protest, *Kookaburra II* was eliminated and the 'bloodbath' predicted by Iain Murray trickled away in a final flurry of protests on the first day of the Defender Finals that resulted in both yachts being thrown out of the race.

From then on *Kookaburra III*'s flight towards victory was unstoppable. Parry's yacht took five straight races off Bond's *Australia IV* in the best-of-nine series, earning Iain Murray and his starting helmsman/mainsheet trimmer, Peter Gilmour, the right to meet Dennis Conner in the America's Cup.

There were suggestions that Ben Lexcen had in fact altered

the Bond boat in mid series, and that she was actually going slower than before, but it's more likely that the *Kookaburras* were also getting faster. Observers who had been impressed by *Australia IV*'s earlier speed felt she looked lacklustre. Whatever the truth of the matter, *Australia IV* was a shadow of her former self. With her starting helmsman at the wheel for the pre-start manoeuvres, *Kookaburra III* never looked threatened.

The final race of the Defender Trials had all the drama of a slow day at a county cricket ground. *Australia IV* was effectively out of the race before it began. The 26-year-old Gilmour forced *Australia IV* the wrong side of the committee boat marking the inner limit of the starting line and was 36 seconds into the race by the time *Australia IV* had recovered.

In light winds *Australia IV* could do nothing to recover and finished 55 seconds adrift. As *Kookaburra*'s supporters clambered aboard for the run back to Fremantle, *Australia IV*'s crew hung their heads.

Later that evening both boats nosed into the Royal Perth's dock for a brief farewell party. The victors were toasted, speeches were made but the atmosphere was subdued. Parry said a few words and handed over to Bond. As the crews lined up along the decks of the two yachts, Bond put on a brave face and prepared to make the best of it. 'Kevin has an awesome responsibility. We won it for Australia, now don't you lose it. . . . If Kevin doesn't defend it, we'll go and get it back.'

So the People's Favourite began his not-so-subtle transformation into Heroic Loser. It was wonderful to behold. Even in Parry's moment of triumph, Bond was determined to have his share of the limelight. Only that morning, his $AUS 1 billion deal to buy Kerry Packer's media empire had hit the headlines. Bond was now owner of the most powerful TV network in the country. Reporters had been trying all day to reach him as he watched the racing out on Gage Roads. At the press conference that evening the stage was set for a Bond benefit. Again he challenged Parry. 'We'll be flying the kangaroo flag proudly. . . . If you lose the Cup Kevin, I suppose we'll have the job of winning it back . . . so don't lose it. . . .'

Parry reacted graciously at first, but there was anger in his eyes; haltingly he launched into an extraordinary attack. All the anger and frustration of the previous months flooded out. How dare Bond suggest that Parry and the 100 members of the Taskforce syndicate were anything other than determined to defend the Cup? How dare he suggest that *Australia IV* was anything other than the slower boat? *Kookaburra III* had won fairly and squarely: 'The fact that you were not good enough in the competition is just a fact of life', he said. 'I don't think it's necessary to stand up today at the Royal Perth and say, "Well, we won it, and if you lose it we'll have to go out and get it back". I think it's childish, unnecessary and unworthy of his previous efforts.'

Parry then contended that the Boxing Kangaroo was not Bond's exclusive property and that it 'belongs to all of us'. He then turned his attention to the media coverage of the event. 'I think it was a marvellous coup that Alan's bought Packer's stations. Over the past week it has been impossible to watch the Defence races on Channel 9. I'm not interested in bulldust newspaper campaigns to denigrate our efforts. I think the people who sailed on *Australia IV* deserve every praise.... I would have hated to be in their position. The truth speaks for itself, and sometimes I wonder if the media speaks for itself.'

It was a graceless end to the Defence campaign and Australia was not amused. There was immense sympathy for the defeated Bond. Leader writers had a field day. 'Why doesn't Parry go out and buy a .38? He could save himself $20 million.', wrote John Hamilton in the *West Australian*. 'How do you resurrect a featherless *Kookaburra* from a public relations disaster?' The answer seemed obvious – hire Bond's Warren Jones; a serious suggestion at the time.

Bond's remarks about his having to win the Cup back if *Kookaburra* failed looked even less credible when he announced, a day or so before the Cup itself, that he was going ahead with a $US 7.5 million deal to sell both *Australia III* and *Australia IV* to a Japanese syndicate and that, moreover, he was backing the Japanese to the tune of $US 1.3 million. 'It will encourage the sport of 12 Metre racing to bring Japan up to the status of a viable contender.' A better reason, perhaps, was given in his next remark: 'We want to sell our beer there, so there is a commercial reason as well.'

As for challenging again for the Cup, Bond said that 'in all probability', he wouldn't.

The next bombshell to burst off Fremantle was the announcement by Michael Fay that the Kiwi syndicate would flout convention and help the Defender in the run-up to the Cup. Although the offer of *Kiwi Magic* as a trial horse to the *Kooka-*

burra syndicate was condemned by Malin Burnham of the *Stars & Stripes* syndicate, Fay stood his ground.

Conner's earlier allegations about cheating over the use of glass-fibre in the yacht had fizzled out with Lloyd's ruling that the yacht was legal, but the bad taste remained. Burnham had suggested privately that the fairest thing to do would be to remain neutral and to watch from the sidelines: 'It's against the principles that I believe in', he said, stony-faced, 'but no big deal. I certainly understand the historical relationship between New Zealand and Australia.'

Although the Kiwis did not give the *Kookaburras* any technical support, the offer of *Kiwi Magic* was gratefully accepted. Fay's decision reflected the opinion of the majority of New Zealanders, many of whom had backed the $15 million campaign. Fay also had two precedents to support his case; *Australia IV* trialling with *Stars & Stripes* and the *Kookaburras'* sparring matches with *America II*. The *Kookaburra* syndicate could see nothing improper in the gesture. 'When the Anzacs put up a fight', said a Taskforce director, 'they usually win.' Burnham accused Fay of bad faith and of breaking a gentlemen's agreement between the Challengers. Fay responded by saying that the Kiwi team would not have felt comfortable helping Conner.

Thus *KZ7* brought to the *Kookaburra* camp the detailed knowledge of eight races against *Stars & Stripes*. 'In New Zealand and in Australia our supporters are now solidly behind the Australian Defence of the Cup', said Fay.

With the *Kookaburras* and *Kiwi Magic* trialling on Gage Roads, and Conner and his support boat circling curiously around to try to pick up any secrets, the stage was set for the showdown between America and Australia. If the Kiwi support was useful, more help was finally on the way as Perth's battling millionaires settled their differences.

The final, amusing, twist to the tale came a week later. Peace, of a kind, broke out on Australia Day as the two Defence syndicates buried the hatchet, exchanged battle flags and united behind the Defence of the America's Cup.

While Dennis Conner engaged in psychological warfare at sea, unfurling a buxom new spinnaker that was instantly dubbed Dolly Parton, Bond took advantage of Parry's absence by taking the wind out of his sails in a gesture that bore all the classic hallmarks of Warren Jones.

With Parry in Peking, signing a Chinese TV deal, Bond called a press conference. All would be smoothed over, the press were assured. Bond's offer of help to the *Kookaburra* syndicate still stood, and whatever the differences between their leaders, the crews of the boats were actively supporting each other. *Kookaburra* was experimenting with *Australia IV*'s radical new genniker sail, and every resource was being pooled. And to cap it all the Bond syndicate announced that it was to become a sponsor of the *Kookaburras*. A cheque for $AUS 100,000 was handed over to a bemused Ken Court, Deputy Chairman of Taskforce '87. 'We want the best Defence', beamed Bond and announced that the Boxing Kangaroo flag – incidentally a trademark belonging to the Bond syndicate – would be made available to the *Kookaburra* yacht. Iain Murray, arriving late from final trials between the two *Kookaburras*, was in no position to refuse.

Whether it was a spontaneous gesture or not, Parry would return to find Bond's flag atop both his base camp and his boat – a flag that had become synonymous with *Australia II*'s Newport victory in 1983.

But there was unity behind the Defence at last. Iain Murray would not be fighting Dennis Conner alone. The rest would be up to the men who ground the winches and trimmed the sails.

CHAPTER NINE

Top Gun

Stuart Alexander/ Adrian Morgan

General MacArthur's words: 'I shall return' were tailor-made for Dennis Conner, the 44-year-old helmsman who came from defeat and humiliation in 1983 to win back the America's Cup. Four years ago he carried around his neck a label which, to most Americans, ranks lower than any other: loser. By the time *Stars & Stripes* had beaten *Kookaburra III* in the last race on 4 February 1987 he was a national hero, symbol of America's sporting pride.

Those who thought they'd seen the back of the Big Man from San Diego as he shuffled tearfully backstage at the end of the emotional final race press conference in Newport's old Armory building were to see him return, his powers behind the wheel of a 12 Metre sharper than ever before. Those who saw him demolish *Kookaburra III* in four straight races witnessed the final episode in a saga that Conner had planned to the last detail and which was to leave him the undisputed champion of 12 Metre racing. Even during those dark days following *Australia II*'s victory, Conner carried the spark of the torch that would light up a nation.

'He's the biggest, meanest sucker in the forest and we want him bad.' Everyone wanted Dennis Conner that summer, and when Warren Jones, manager of Alan Bond's Defence syndicate, picked Conner as the man they most wanted to meet in the America's Cup itself he was expressing a common sentiment in Fremantle during the long, hard Cup months.

Without beating Dennis Conner, an America's Cup campaign is not complete. Even those consigned to oblivion will speak with pride of the day they put one over on Dennis. For 12 years he has been the one against whom 12 Metre sailing was judged.

To the *boulevardiers* on South Terrace, Fremantle, on the lookout for skippers, crews, back-up men, anyone to do with a syndicate, Dennis was the star, the one they wanted to tell their friends they had seen. And they often did. While some crews led a monastic existence during the racing and others were very cliquey, Conner would often hit the town, always immaculate in a blazer with its *Stars & Stripes* badge, happy to be out for a drink or to talk to people, as long as he could keep the contact at arm's length and reasonably short.

In the pursuit of an obsession Dennis could afford only so much time to be nice. As his campaign began to bear fruit, however, Big Bad Dennis, the introverted expert they all loved to hate, emerged slowly from his shell, as his confidence grew.

The defeat in 1983, and the ending of a 132-year run of invincibility presided over by the New York Yacht Club, cost him dear in personal terms. He had spent a frustrating time seeking a fast boat and in *Liberty* knew he did not have one. He had tried all he knew to pull the boat he had up by its bootstraps to deny the faster Australians. That he came so close to denying them was remarkable. Deserted by the New York Yacht Club he was left to face the predatory ranks of reporters alone.

There was to be no New York Yacht Club backing this time for the trip to Fremantle. They did not offer; he would not have accepted. The battle plan for 1987 would be his alone, backed up by a personal bodyguard of close friends and respected allies. Instead, it was his own club, the San Diego Yacht Club which was to sponsor his Challenge and Malin Burnham, a man born to fortune and success, winner at the age of 17 of the Star World Championships in 1945, who was to be the syndicate's rock anchor.

Conner took his campaign to Waikiki in Hawaii, where he could test, train and practise in conditions similar to those he expected to find in Fremantle, and most importantly among fellow Americans. In Hawaii he would find the big breezes, big seas and an altogether more physical kind of racing to the flukey winds and heaving swell he knew so well not only in Newport, Rhode Island, but also in San Diego.

While he was carefully building the programme which would give him the boatspeed he had lacked in 1983, at the same time he was putting together the crew he would need. Letters were sent to every collegiate rowing coach in the United States asking if they could recommend anyone who might be suitable for the testing physical strain of winding the big pedestal winches used to set and adjust the sails.

Over 500 people replied without invitation. Applications were sifted, checks made, and a chosen few invited to make the journey to Hawaii to see how they shaped up. Old hands were called in to work in the team once again, men like Scott Vogel, bowman on *Liberty*, Bill Trenkle, Jon Wright, Tom Whidden, and Kyle Smith. Six of their regular crew were over 30. A number were on their third or fourth America's Cup campaigns. All the *Kookaburra* crew, except 35-year-old Derek Clark, were under 30.

Under the guidance of US Olympic sailing coach Robert Hopkins the candidates were assessed. Could they fit in and command other crew members' respect as well as do the job on the boat, help without being asked ashore, make a contribution to the improvement of the boat and, very important, demonstrate a total will to win the America's Cup?

Like his ultimate rival Iain Murray, Conner ignored the World 12 Metre Championships held at Fremantle in February of 1986, preferring to keep his development programme going, marching along to his own tune and to a timetable set up by the team. By the time he arrived in Fremantle he had tested and evaluated five 12 Metres. He was also a changed man, still obsessed, consumed by the need to win, still with many of the traits which make him such a difficult man to deal with, but with some new attributes, more rounded, able at times to be slightly more relaxed, and looking for more contact and humour.

Conner had learned to spread the burden and was happy to let others be in the forefront, although he would still be at the dock as dawn broke over Fremantle's Fishing Boat Harbour. Of his team, two men stood out; John Marshall, who co-ordinated the design team – Dave Pedrick, Bruce Nelson and Britton Chance – and Tom Whidden. Whidden, his sailmaker ashore and tactician afloat was, most importantly, his friend – a man he could trust, who would play the straight man to Conner's almost boyish humour on stage at the nightly press conferences. In his professional rôle Whidden, soon to become President of North Sails, was invaluable; as a friend, superb. Still, however, Conner had a strong distrust for the press which he has always seen as being too prone to jump to uninformed conclusions. He could occasionally give way to temper: 'If you're so smart, why aren't you up here instead of being down there asking stupid questions', he once snapped from the press conference platform. But he could also display a nice line in self-deprecating humour. In answer to another inane question: 'Do you think a victory by America would restore the nation's prestige after Irangate?', Conner replied: 'I am just a poor sailor, down here to win a sailboat race'. To him that was the bottom line. Beneath the surface Dennis was essentially unchanged. His style became the butt of mimics. His voice has a hesitant quiver to it than can leave you wondering if he will make it to the end of a sentence. He will occasionally take flight into a metaphor, realise halfway through he is uncomfortable with it, and then abandon it, bolting quickly into the safety of stock phrases and answers he knows.

Soon the papers were calling him 'Mr Nice Guy'. It hadn't taken much to achieve the turnaround: giving a local boy who had asked for his autograph a dream ride on *Stars & Stripes*, a few jocular remarks, opening an antiques fair, and donating a $1000 prize he had won to the youth section of the local sailing club. At the press conferences, Conner was ready to clown in outrageous *Stars & Stripes* rugby shirts or josh with the chairman. But the media platform is not his stage. The sea is his stage and the difference is as dramatic as the moment when a swan waddling along the riverbank on big, black, webbed feet takes to the water. Dennis is a big bird and he fits well into a big boat. He looks the part.

Where Conner does feel very much at home on land is in the detailed preparation of his yacht. No idea, however small, is discarded without at least cursory thought. During a conversation with the donnish John Marshall, goes a story, Conner interrupted and obliquely asked: 'Do you think they're fast?' 'What?', said Marshall, confused. 'Do you think they're fast?', he repeated pointing to the goldfish tank. 'No', said Marshall, recovering, 'they're bred to be decorative.' Conner would not give up. 'Yes, but do you think they're fast, you know, the body shape and the fins?' He pointed to the bigger of the fish. Was it perhaps that it reached the food on the surface quicker than the others because it had a better body shape?

Chris Dickson, the skipper of *KZ7*, beaten by Conner for the Challenger slot, once said that if Conner went into a duel with two bullets in his gun to his opponent's one then he would probably shoot the opponent dead with the first bullet. The second would give him the extra edge of confidence he needed.

It is through the preparation of the boat that Conner seeks that extra bullet. Over 400 computer-generated models were tested, of which 40 scale models were built. As *Stars & Stripes* fought through to the Finals her speed increased as the boat was refined and refined. Right up to the last minute the Star Wars steamroller was being optimised for her avenging rôle until Conner was satisfied that he had the weapon he needed to win in the unique wave and wind conditions off Fremantle.

The biggest single surprise was a grooved plastic film, developed by 3M in Minneapolis and applied to the hull between the Challenger Semi-Finals and the Finals. The surface, like that of a gramophone record, reduced friction, it was claimed, by up to 6 per cent. The film's rôle was acknowledged, but played down. But there is no doubt that the etched microgroove 'riblets' helped *Stars & Stripes* significantly, even if only psychologically. A film developed for reducing friction on aircraft bodies, and used to devastating effect by the, hitherto unranked, American Olympic coxed four Silver medal rowing teams at Los Angeles, was the secret weapon in 1987.

Evolved as an upwind flier in winds of over 15 knots, *Stars & Stripes* had one Achilles' heel – downwind in light winds. The riblet coating helped to plug that gap. While Conner was encouraging the opposition to believe that his yacht was slow downwind, he was working on a solution. The boat was already stiff and, thanks to a new plating and framing system employed by her builder, Bob Derecktor, the combination of subtle keel modifications, riblets, new sails and forward mast rake was enough to turn *Stars & Stripes* into a Super 12, as radical a yacht as any seen in Fremantle that year.

In retrospect Conner's progress seemed inevitable. From having won 11 races in the first Round Robin and sharing equal first place with the much-fancied New York Yacht Club's *America II*, and the plastic fantastic New Zealand yacht, Conner slumped slightly in the light winds of November's second Round Robin. At one stage he even said that if the flukey conditions persisted the boat would be in such a bad position they would be home by Thanksgiving. In fact he won seven races and went into the third and crucial series in third position.

America II, on the other hand, peaked too early. The syndicate threw money at her but it made no difference. As other boats began improving, she stopped. Even Buddy Melges, the 51-year-old Wizard of Zenda, Star Gold medallist and the oldest skipper there began to give some of the fancied runners a few scary moments, cranking *Heart of America* up to new heights.

Dennis had no problem making second place and a berth in the Semi-Finals, though he conceded another race to New Zealand. In the Semi-Finals he drew Tom Blackaller; Blackaller whose quick tongue and ready wit seemed so different to Conner's style. Brilliant Blackaller, with his playboy looks, motor racing background and dislike for the deadly serious approach, so nearly proved his point with the radical, twin-ruddered *USA*. Once or twice Blackaller squeezed in front, but eventually he went down 4–0 to Conner's machine. 'To beat Dennis', he once said, 'you have to crawl all over his dead body.'

The story of Conner's matches with the Kiwis is told elsewhere. In many ways it was the climax of the Cup Summer: *Kiwi Magic*, bird-like and agile, against the dragster. The dragster won, but the New Zealanders gave Conner the toughest racing of all. He was glad to have them out of the way at long last. When Michael Fay announced that *Kiwi Magic* would be trialling with the *Kookaburras*, Conner was disappointed. Although the Taskforce skipper, Iain Murray, claimed that *Kookaburra* was faster in those trials, there is a lingering suspicion that the New Zealand yacht gave them a shock. Conner gatecrashed the trials. What he learnt gave him even greater confidence.

A few months before, Ben Lexcen had said: 'Conner's boats [are] too short, too stubby, too agricultural. They're nothing flash. I mean they're not rocket ships to the moon. They're just ordinary. In fact they seem to be less than ordinary.' There was nothing ordinary about the final, fully-tuned gunsmoke-blue yacht from San Diego.

By the time Conner met the Kiwis he had the backing of all the other American Syndicates that had fallen by the wayside. Just before the Final began, Conner also had a new mainsail made in the first 300 yards of a composite cloth using three exotic materials – he was still driving the search for more boatspeed ahead. The New York Yacht Club's *America II* donated mainsails and spinnakers and a lightweight mainsail from Blackaller was to be used to devastating effect in her first race against Iain Murray. The rocketship had uncorked her boosters. Those who had seen her falter in the first rounds, and fight back in light weather to the top four in the Challenger Trials, could hardly believe she was the same boat.

At the measuring before the Finals, Iain Murray made a prophetic comment: 'Their boat is different to ours', he said, 'so I suppose someone's right and someone's wrong.'

Meanwhile Conner set about working on his light air speed. It was to pay off handsomely in the first race, dispelling once and for all the myth that *Stars & Stripes* was simply a heavy weather boat. Murray and his young crew looked stagestruck. Conner chose the left-hand side of the course, protected it as the wind shifted 20 degrees in his favour, then a massive 40 degrees, to round the top mark one minute 15 seconds ahead. *Kookaburra III* never stood a chance, even when the wind freshened to 18 knots in mid race. Conner maintained a loose cover, ignoring Murray's attempts to engage in a tacking duel, though the latter did pick up 39 seconds on the second beat. The margin at the finish was one minute 41 seconds, although Murray could draw some comfort from the fact that *Stars & Stripes*, once ahead, was never more than one minute 20 seconds up. Of the wind shift Conner said: 'It was nothing we really planned.' It must have seemed like the luck of the Devil to the 28-year-old Sydneysider whose misfortune it was to meet the Master in his first America's Cup race.

By the second day the Cup seemed to be heading inexorably towards Southern California as *Kookaburra*'s Defence crumbled in high winds. In contrast to the Saturday race, the wind blew with a vengeance. *Kookaburra*'s 26-year-old starting helmsman, Peter Gilmour from Fremantle, drove the golden-hulled yacht into pole position before the gun. But as *Kookaburra* took Conner on a long drag to the left-hand side of the course it soon became apparent that *Stars & Stripes* was eating relentlessly into Murray's lead with every blast of hot air that hurtled in from the Indian Ocean. Fourteen minutes into the race and Conner was level. Murray tacked away in search of better fortune to the right, found none and the race was over. She trailed the American by 12 seconds at the first mark, slipped 29 seconds further into the red at the bottom and was one minute 14 seconds in deficit as *Stars & Stripes* surfed to the wing mark. A genniker and staysail supplied by Alan Bond's *Australia IV* were broken out but she could find none of that vaunted downwind speed. Instead she looked outclassed, her bows swept constantly by green water, her motion in the big seas uncomfortable compared to that of the blue boat. Murray had very few options. With the wind steady from the south-west, Conner kept *Stars & Stripes* between the mark and his opponent, supremely confident in conditions for which his training in Hawaii had left him well prepared. 'We expected a strong performance by *Stars & Stripes*', said Murray, 'and that's what we got, but we'd prefer not to sail against her in those winds again.'

Somebody thought a bomb scare would liven up the third race. After a brilliant opening gambit by Gilmour, *Kookaburra* found herself defending the right side of the line and crossed ahead after one tack. Twice more they clashed, each time with the Australian's lead slightly diminished. At the fourth meeting Conner ducked Murray's stern, powered up and broke through *Kookaburra*'s covering tack. From then on *Stars & Stripes* was unassailable, sliding downwind to a comfortable 57 second lead which she stretched to one minute 46 at the gun.

The bomb scare nearly stopped the race in the final stages. Following a tip-off to Kevin Parry *Kookaburra*'s chase boat ranged alongside and offered to take the crew off. Trailing badly at this stage Murray's position was hopeless. Nevertheless they decided to stay put. ' "You've got a bomb on board" ', recounted Iain Murray. 'Our immediate response was, "What's the bad news?" We thought perhaps we'd like to see what life was like after 12 Metre racing', he joked grimly. 'We didn't think if the bomb went off it would affect the race.'

With lighter winds forecast Conner called a lay day. It was Murray's last chance to find a little extra speed. On the fourth day, five minutes before the gun, and despite the fact that sharks had been spotted in the waters the previous day – attracted no doubt by the waste from the enormous armada of spectator boats – *Kookaburra* had divers over the side applying a special go-faster coating. At the gun Peter Gilmour engaged Conner in the fiercest pre-start manoeuvres of the series. The blue boat weaved and ducked between the spectator fleet in a thrilling display of match racing, trying to shake off the *Kookaburra*. With 30 seconds to go the two boats were locked together and it seemed that Conner would be forced over early. With just two seconds to the gun Conner stalled, *Kookaburra* slowed, and *Stars & Stripes* was away. It was a display of nautical pyrotechnics that will be remembered long after *Kookaburra*'s sad finale.

At the first mark Conner had edged out by 26 seconds; at the second 22. By the second windward mark Conner was 42 seconds ahead. *Kookaburra* sailed faster than she had ever sailed before. She had found an edge, but it was not enough. *Kookaburra* gained just one second more on the reach to the bottom mark. From then on the margin increased inexorably, despite Murray's attempts to draw Conner into a tacking duel.

'How many ways are there to say that *Stars & Stripes* was faster?', asked a journalist watching the race. It was a brutal comment, but essentially true. Upwind and down, in all conditions, Conner's yacht had the measure of the Australians. *Kookaburra* was ultimately no match for a weapon like that in the hands of a master swordsman. Even as Dennis Conner punched upwind to a one minute 59 second victory on the final beat of the race the San Diego Yacht Club announced that it would be hosting the next Defence. Australia had kept the Cup for just four years. In that time the event had changed out of all recognition. Australia's victory had breathed new life into the contest, her first Defence on the superb waters off Fremantle had taken the art of 12 Metre racing to new levels of expertise. But amidst the disappointment and the elation few people doubted Conner's right. The America's Cup was in safe hands again. Never again would the country after whose famous schooner the Cup was named be caught napping. The master sailor had reclaimed a nation's rightful inheritance.

But the Aussies never give up: A sign on the docks of Fremantle that evening read: *Boomerangs always come back, so will the America's Cup.*

POSTSCRIPT

East of Cunderdin
A Letter to a Friend

Jonathan Eastland

Bulong, W.A.
February, 1987

Dear Sid,

G'day mate! I'd have gotten to this a lot sooner but for a couple of things that brushed by me and stuck like the proverbial cow-pat to a wool sock. Even now, I'm not at all certain that any of this will reach you by the time I've trenched out a few hectares of bush in search of that elusive golden nugget, but never mind. I'll press on in the hope that Bruce here will meet up with the posty on his next foray into Kal.

So much has happened since last September. Pardon me if I lose a few threads here and there; hopefully we can darn those in next time round if you've still got that fifth tucked away in the dipping shed.

The flight out from England was torturous; the first thing I did was to go to a travel agent and have the carrier changed for the homeward passage, whenever it came. You were right about the weather. It was pouring buckets when we landed. I'd spent all my change in the Singapore transit lounge and didn't have a bean to give the cabbie on the ride into Perth. I called Barry about four in the morning, but he wasn't too keen on picking us up, said something about having a skinful the previous evening and wasn't sure if he still had wheels. We all just collapsed into a hotel that first night and slept and slept. Then Russell came over from Sydney and drove us to the mansion in Fremantle. It took about a week to stop waking up at four in the morning. I used to think going to Newport was a bind, but 23 hours!

The house was great; perched up on a hill in East Freo' with a view of the ocean if you cared to walk out into the middle of the street. Everyone had a room, decorated with pressed, zinc-coated ceilings, and it was hardly ever too hot in the day. A verandah went all the way round too, and it must have been great to sit out there in 1906. Of course, there wasn't a house for miles around in those days. Now it's just another suburb. Gradually the house filled up with blunts and monkeys and we held several huge barbecues for friends and media orphans.

Luckily there was a large pool in the back garden. I say luckily because the only time you could get a swim on the local beaches without fear of being sandblasted was before breakfast. The wind was so strong most days that it was impossible to enjoy the beach for its own sake. You'd go home after an hour and your eyeballs felt as if they'd been worked on by a glass etcher. No, no, the 'sand groper' has nothing to do with beaches. That came about because most of this part of the world is a giant sand pit; the natives got dubbed sand gropers by residents of the eastern States where the land is mostly lush and green.

To begin with there were not very many of us here when the 'Cup' caper started in October. Some were locals but the majority had come in from overseas and set up camp pretty much as we had. The press office was a huge World War II boom defence building, lately a hockey stadium off the aptly named 'Fleet Street' near the docks entrance, dubbed 'The Media Centre'. The organisers had done a terrific job turning the place into a vast hall full of desks, telephones and computers in order to accommodate an expected flood of over 2000 journalists (blunts). The photographers (monkeys) were relegated to an equally well-equipped portacabin annexe manned by a team from Fuji-Hanimex. Being the largest agency, we had our own office there, but even that started to become a little cramped towards the end. The place filled up with groupies and Cup freaks from all over. You should have seen them.

One fellow from a noted sporting journal proudly showed me about 200 Kodachrome boxes full of slides he'd shot one day – a non-race day too. When I asked him why on earth he needed to shoot so much stuff, he said: 'Well, we need to bracket exposure and bracket the focus'. I cowered into submission. Bracketing focus? What happened to the single-lens reflex that came along 30 years before to put an end to blurred, out-of-focus pictures? 'Bracket focus' was patently a new technique.

When I told the boys back at the farm, we had a serious sit-down amongst the tinnies. The real problem was that the sheer logistics of editing 500 rolls of film a day would require extra personnel. Kempstaff said he knew a local golfer who'd done some spare-time editing for a local rag called the *Challenge Gazette*. 'The Boy', our own darkroom technician, would pitch in as well, but we'd still need two more working flat out on the corridor lightboxes if we were ever to have a hope of moving the first picture of the day before midnight the next – midday in New York and four in the afternoon in London.

There was always the possibility too, that Reuters or News Ltd, or even some of the newspapers working at our end of the building would become suspicious and then they'd all start holding the finger down. Fuji would have to install six more auto film processors and bring in extra staff to cope. It was pretty soon obvious that we'd all end up being strangled by miles of rampant polyester. It was a good idea though, so we put in a formal request to New York for a six-storey portacabin of our own for the 1990/91 event wherever it might be held. Finally, a message came up on the wire a few days later asking for more details of the focus bracket and who made it.

While all this and more filled the lay days, and the evenings were spent wiring pictures well into the small hours, the yacht racing went on and on, on Gage Roads. Once we'd been there a few weeks, the weather became more easily predictable in the absence of accurate forecasts. We knew by then that the sea breeze came in in the afternoon and why. The so-called 'Fremantle Doctor' is a wind that blows from seaward as the land mass heats up and creates a vacuum as the hot air rises. I discovered that this daily doctorial prescription which everyone raves about was never called 'Doctor' by the locals of 1897. The 'Fremantle Docker', however, makes much more sense; in the old days sailing ship masters would lay at anchor out on the roads during the morning and bring their vessels gently up the Swan River in the afternoon.

With access to two cray boats, a launch and a helicopter, you could hardly say we were short of positions. Spoilt for choice would be more accurate. A great monster of an aluminium barge called *Bismark* carried the Australian TV Pool camera and staffer from each of the agencies plus a *Time* man. Once or twice the going got a little rough and people would get thrown around, beaten up and bruised.

Barry Stevens opted one day to take his leisure on the *Sorrento*, along with about 25 others, but it was one of those sloppy days with big swells and 25 knots of wind. While the skipper backed up to the weather mark for a few close-ups, Barry was snooked into a garbage box; when he finally extricated himself from the remains of glad-wrapped prawn rolls, he was pitched to the port rail, smashing two ribs and lacerating both arms. Another day, as he lurched forward for the classic America's Cup crossing pose, his large and expensive telephoto lens was disintegrated against the bulwark of the *Bismark*.

Young Stephen Holland, an import from Sydney, was originally hired as a darkroom technician, a printer in simple English. His enthusiasm, however, showed no bounds and after he had produced a run of creditable feature pictures, he was armed with proper equipment and given the harbour boat trip each morning. This sidebar assignment was intended to generate personality pictures of the combatants who steered the great winged chariots into battle on the Indian Ocean.

One morning, 'The Boy's' own chariot, a 16 ft runabout with an 80 hp outboard, awaited his arrival on the media landing-stage, a mere stone's throw from our office. To board the boat, one had to negotiate a 12-rung vertical ladder with equipment slung around one's arms or neck. That particular morning, a slight swell was running into the harbour and as Stephen tentatively put a foot out to board the launch, a rogue swell whacked the stern out. He slipped rapidly to the bottom rung, entering the water first in slow motion and then with gathering speed as the weight of two cameras with heavy lenses pulled him downward like a ship's anchor. He said that time passed slowly; he thought there wasn't much chance of returning to the surface. All around was inky blackness. He doesn't recall how long it took to get back up, but he did and walked into the office looking like the proverbial drowned rat, ashen grey, sodden and very quiet. The cameras were written off, but his indecision as to whether to dump them or not saved the lenses and the corporation a hefty bill.

Stephen was given his nickname by Dennis Conner following a meeting between the two accidentally engineered by Betsy

Whidden, wife of *Stars & Stripes'* tactician, Tom, whom
Stephen had befriended while trying to accommodate a special
request from a newspaper in coldest Connecticut.

A simple family gathering around the Christmas tree had
been asked for. Stephen duly arrived at the Whiddens'
residence at the prescribed time and discovered Dennis dishing
out presents to the whole *Stars & Stripes* crew and shore gang.
Stephen began shooting frames of the man most people were
predicting would take the 'Auld Mug' back to the United
States of America.

Dennis apparently had not had a good day and perhaps
spurred on by recollections of an earlier picture of himself
snapped dozing in a café by the same photographer now present,
made a graphic indication of how he thought young Stephen
should make his exit. The Whiddens later apologised for Mr
Conner's behaviour and when Dennis next saw the inimitable
Barry, he suggested that the next time 'The Boy' was sent to
do a man's job, he be properly equipped with a real camera,
not an Instamatic. In recompense, Stephen was invited to go
sailing on *US-55* and thence began a wonderful relationship
between the man and boy, the Whiddens and the crew of the
Challenger. That will explain, Sid, all those 'on board' pictures
in the papers back home.

As time ticked on, one began to sympathise with the local
shopkeepers who had invested between them what must have
amounted to millions of dollars' worth of America's Cup kitsch,
knick-knacks and souvenirs. This in addition to their normal
stock kept essentially for the needs of the locals. No doubt there
that someone had been overly optimistic in their estimates of
the new passing trade and when it would arrive. It barely
scratched the pavements. All that stuff about tourists
generating billions of extra dollars dissolved like sugar in
simmering syrup.

Frank Ellis, proprietor of a T-shirt emporium complained
bitterly that piles of fashionable collectors' garb and other Cup
memorabilia were being passed up in favour of a burger at 'Fast
Eddy's', but you could hardly sympathise with the hustlers
who had gatecrashed this old outport in a bid for a fast buck.
The Royal Perth Yacht Club itself was possibly to blame for
propagating the idea that fortunes would, not 'might be' made.
When this circus first began way back in 1983, its officers were
the first to agree that the flagpoles outside its headquarters

should be leased to the highest bidder. The hype just
snowballed from then on.

And the yachts sailed on and on. There were times when it
seemed the racing would never end; I even thought fondly of
the ice-age going on back in Europe while I was basking in 33
degrees of sunshine from my helicopter perch over the yachts.
That must have been the day my brain stopped working; shaken
loose by countless hours of buffeting and rotor whirling, a
noise heightened by wearing a headset through which came the
constant clatter of a Lycoming air-cooled engine and the
chatter of nine or ten other pilots all intent on putting their
cameramen in the 'right' position. There was never time to
write notes to the pilot when a spinnaker shredded 500 feet
below.

It must have been about then too when it dawned on me
that I hadn't seen anything the other side of the Darling Range.
So we took off as soon as the Christmas break dawned; headed
east along the highway for an outpost at the end of a 400-mile
freshwater pipeline. Gliding down the inland side of the range
we hit the wheatfields; golden vistas for miles. Joe Crook,
who'd stopped at Burracoppin for a wet on his way south to
Noombenburry Rock, said the economy was wretched but he
wished Maggie well. He'd been a 'Cocky' for 30 years and the
way he looked, he'd still be a part of the landscape 30 years
on. He was the first real Australian I'd seen in three months.

The pipeline runs all the way from Perth to Kalgoorlie. A
man called C. Y. O'Conner devoted the better part of his life
to building it. He ended his own life after months of persecution
and speculation about whether the water would run out or run
back. Here we were, enjoying the comforts of modern technology on a seven-hour drive, which would have taken the
pioneers of this country weeks, sometimes months, by horse,
camel or cart.

Kalgoorlie is one of those places you either love or hate. I
loved it. If you took out all the cars, you could imagine how
it was back in those Gold Rush days of yore. The Old Australia
Hotel is pretty much how it was in 1897, as is the Palace on
the opposite side of the street. We sat on the hotel's wooden
verandah and silently watched the sun go down, the old
Victorian buildings changing colour every minute, just as they
had done every day for a hundred years.

Kal is a boisterous, pioneering huddle of shops and drinking holes. It could die tomorrow, just as its one-time larger sister Coolgardie has done 40 clicks west; all but two of its 75 hotels gone, erased by fire or tempest and a seam of yellow ore that just plain fizzled out. Kal still has 23 of its one-time 90-odd hotels. We filled our stomachs to bursting in the York with turkey and Christmas Fayre as good as Mother cooked. Someone played a piano and the tin ceiling reverberated to the sound of coarsely-sung carols.

We met good people here. Just ordinary folk happy to share a beer and conversation in the gardens of their fossickers' shacks. Lennie Pearce, Robbie Wakefield, 'Bluey'; relics of a lifetime of hard living in a hard land, their generosity untainted by the bickerings of obsessed yachtsmen and the greed of corporate huckstery. The Cup never got this far.

There's more of course. Like the day we found the graves of prospectors, their wives and children just by here in the bush at Bulong. White stones glaring in the noonday sun as if they had been planted yesterday. These people had come from the bogs of Ireland and the smog of Manchester at the turn of the century in the quest for a dream; their short lives were beleaguered by the incessant attention of flies, lack of proper hygiene, sickness, accidents and eventually an unnoticed death under this unrelenting sun.

A hundred years from now, Sid, those white stone epitaphs will still be glinting in the sunlight. We returned to the coast and finished the war. The day after it finished I watched as the cleaners dumped four and a half months' worth of clippings into the council garbage truck. I expect you'll soon be using yours to light the fire with. Fremantle heaved a sigh of relief and went back to being an outport, its next high point a visit from the *Al Yasran* taking 127,000 sheep for the three-week voyage north to the Middle East.

We packed up and shipped out back here. I've got my $30 nugget hammer and sunsets across the glade for as long as I want. You can write care of the post office in Kal. Someone will bring it out one day.

Yours ever

Harry

The Competitors

DEFENDERS

Syndicate/Yacht/Club/Skippers

America's Cup Defence
Australia III
Australia IV
Royal Perth YC
Colin Beashel and
Gordon Lucas

Taskforce '87
Kookaburra II
Kookaburra III
Royal Perth YC
Iain Murray and Peter
Gilmour

South Australian
Challenge
South Australia
Royal South Australia
Yacht Squadron
Phil Thompson

Eastern Australia
Defence Syndicate
Steak 'n' Kidney
Royal Sydney Yacht
Squadron
Fred Neill

CHALLENGERS
(France, Italy, United
States, Britain, New
Zealand, Canada)

Syndicate/Yacht/Club/Skippers

Sail America Foundation
Stars & Stripes
San Diego YC
Dennis Conner

America II Syndicate
America II
New York YC
John Kolius

Eagle Challenge
Eagle
Newport Harbour YC
Rod Davis

Heart of America Syndicate
Heart of America
Chicago YC
Buddy Melges

Golden Gate Challenge
USA
St Francis YC
Tom Blackaller

Courageous Challenge
Courageous IV
Yale Corinthian YC
Dave Vietor

British America's Cup
Challenges
White Crusader
Royal Thames YC
Harry Cudmore

Challenge Kis
French Kiss
Société des Régates
Rochelaises
Marc Pajot

Challenge France
Challenge France
Société Nautique de
Marseille
Yves Pajot

Consorzio Azzurra
Azzurra
YC Costa Smeralda
Mauro Pelaschier

Consorzio Italia
Italia
YC Italiano
Aldo Migliaccio

Canada II Challenge
Canada II
Royal Nova Scotia Yacht
Squadron
Terry Nielson

BNZ New Zealand Challenge
New Zealand
Royal New Zealand
Yacht Squadron
Chris Dickson

The selection of the Challenger for the 1987 America's Cup was based on the results of the Louis Vuitton Trials which began on 5 October 1986. A series of three Round Robin races produced the four yachts which met in the Semi-Finals between 28 December and 7 January 1987. The Finals between the winning two yachts took place on 13 January. The Louis Vuitton Cup winner then met the defending yacht, chosen in a similar series of selection trials, in the America's Cup itself which started on 31 January 1987.

Challengers were only allowed to enter one yacht, but had the option of switching during the lower scoring preliminary Round Robin series if their initial choice proved a failure. The defending syndicates, however, were allowed to enter as many yachts as they wanted.

APPENDIX II

The Race Course

It is quite impossible to lay down a 'race track' on the sea, like a Formula One circuit. In yacht racing the competitors sail anti-clockwise around buoys anchored to the sea bed. Between these fixed marks the yachts can take any course they like. Each tries to find the fastest way to the next mark; in yacht racing, due to the vagaries of the wind and the need to keep your opponent in sight, that is not always the shortest or straightest line.

The triangular America's Cup course is about 24 miles long as the crow flies. Races started near the Fairway Landfall Buoy marking the entrance to the shipping lane into Fremantle Harbour, about 7 miles away to the south east. Unlike the course off Newport, Rhode Island, home of the America's Cup until 1983, the course was within viewing distance of the shore between the Rottnest Island and the mainland.

The starting line is an imaginary line between a committee boat and a buoy at the 'bottom' of the course and aligned exactly at right angles to the prevailing wind direction. Ten minutes before the designated starting time a gun is fired. The two yachts head towards each other, one from the committee boat end, the other from the buoy end and engage in a series of pre-start manoeuvres, like boxers shaping up for a fight. In the ten-minute period leading up to the gun fired to signal the start of the race the two boats try their utmost to establish a tactical advantage over their rival.

The America's Cup course can best be described as either 'sausages' or 'triangles' (see p. 125). The first leg is 3.25 miles long and is called the windward leg because it is set directly into the wind. To reach the 'top' mark, or windward mark, therefore, the yachts must tack or zigzag into the wind. So the actual distance sailed is far greater than the straight-line 3.25 miles.

At the 'top' mark the yachts turn 180° and head back down the way they came, rounding a mark at the 'bottom', called the leeward mark, before repeating the first leg ('sausage'). Then they head off to the left to a buoy completing the triangle, the wing mark, rounding it and heading back towards the bottom mark ('triangle'). Three more legs, round the windward and leeward marks, bring them to the finishing line; eight legs in all.

If the wind changes during the race, the race officers can physically up anchor and 'move' any of the buoys to keep the 'sausage' directly aligned with the prevailing wind direction. If a buoy is moved, to avoid the yachts heading towards a non-existent mark, they are notified of the new compass course to follow to the 'new' buoy.

Conditions on the race course can change dramatically during the three or so hours it takes to complete all eight legs. As the land heats up during the day a strong south-westerly wind, known locally as the Fremantle Doctor, is sucked in from the sea. A yacht holding an early advantage can have the tables turned as the new breeze sets in.

The eight-leg course is not only a test of boatspeed and tactics, therefore, but also one of endurance and stamina. Winning the pre-start manoeuvres is important, but the course allows plenty of scope for a trailing yacht to catch up and pass the early leader if she loses the tiniest bit of concentration.

Seven mark roundings put a big premium on crew work and sail handling, while the windward legs can be an exhausting battle of attack and counter attack as the heavy yachts are zigzagged up the course.

Tactics

First leg upwind: 3.25nm. After winning the pre-start manoeuvres the leading boat tries to keep the other in her wind shadow, dominating her opponent and responding to any threats by keeping between her and the next mark.

Second leg downwind: 3.25nm. Now it's the chance for the trailing yacht to blanket the yacht ahead, whittling her lead away until she is within striking distance.

Third leg upwind: 3.25nm. The second test of tactics and crew stamina. The leading yacht must stave off determined attacks from her opponent who may also be throwing in dummy tacks to wrong foot her and gain an advantage.

Fourth leg reach: 2.3nm. Supreme test of spinnaker work, especially in strong winds. Little change in position unless the trailing boat can eke out to windward and take her opponent's wind, or sneak inside her at the wing mark. A good gybe here can make all the difference.

Fifth leg reach: 2.3nm. Both yachts will keep their spinnakers drawing to the last minute before dropping and heading back up the beat to the 'top' mark.

Sixth leg upwind: 3.25nm. By now the crew will be tiring as the trailing yacht tries another determined attack, attempting to force a hasty move that could result in gear failure.

Seventh leg downwind: 3.25nm. An opportunity to come from behind as the breeze freshens later in the day. The relative positions at the last mark will be crucial to the final leg and the outcome of the race itself.

Eighth leg upwind: 3.25nm. The climax of the race – the last chance for the loser to break cover. The leading skipper will match his opponent tack for tack to keep between him and the finish line. The final tack for the line will be crucial, especially if the yachts are close. Many races have been lost on the last 100 yards.

The Start

Although the triangular Olympic-style course was designed to test the yachts on all points of sailing, and allow plenty of opportunity for the trailing yacht to fight back, winning the start is vital.

The object of the game is to cross the line ahead of the other yacht just as the gun fires, and in a position to dictate terms. The rules of yacht racing at all times give one or other yacht right of way in order to avoid collisions. The rules are a two-edged weapon. Match racing skippers use them to threaten their opponent and force him to give way. Disqualification awaits the skipper who fails to give way. It's a game of bluff and counter-bluff, controlled aggression, sharp manoeuvring and split second decisions.

Ten minutes before the start of the race, like boxers shaping up for a fight, the two yachts may head towards each other from opposite ends of the line. But just as often one skipper will wait for his opponent to 'come and get him', hoping he will make a mistake in his approach that will allow him to spin round and tag onto his tail – a classic pre-start ploy.

Now begins an elaborate game of nerve as the skippers strive to find a way to trap their opponent in a nautical arm lock from which they can control the first vital leg of the course, upwind to the 'top' mark. The trailing skipper will stick like a leech to the stern of the yacht ahead; his rival trying every trick he knows to lose his 'tail', and turn the tables. He can duck and weave, in an attempt to outmanoeuvre his opponent. And if that fails he may try to 'scrape' his tormentor off by sailing within inches of a spectator boat like a horse trying to unseat a troublesome rider on an overhanging branch or gate post. He can even stop his yacht dead in her tracks, head to the wind, playing a waiting game, hoping he can spin round and break free.

At five minutes before the start the yachts may be some way from the line still, engrossed in their duel. But the tacticians aboard will be keeping a careful note of how far away the line is and how long it would take to reach it. At some point one or other will break off and head for the line. The yacht that was trailing is now in a position to force the pace, even to the extent of pushing the other across the line prematurely, in which case she must duck back and start again, losing vital seconds.

The Beat

Once clear of the line the advantage lies with the yacht that has managed to control the pre-start manoeuvres. She will ideally be slightly ahead, with the wind streaming off her sails right into the path of the yacht behind. This 'dirty' wind plays havoc with her opponent's sail settings and sooner or later the trailing yacht will have to tack to find clean wind or she will lose ground inexorably.

The leading boat will inevitably tack as soon as she sees her opponent trying to break clear in order to keep her in safely tucked up in her dirty wind astern. Both the attacking and 'covering' yacht will be trying to dictate the timing of the tacks to take advantage of any shift in the wind.

If the skipper of the attacking boat manages to time his moves to coincide with favourable wind shifts he may soon begin to overhaul the leading yacht, breaking out of the wind shadow and edging up closer to the direction of the true wind. The leading yacht can respond by 'luffing' towards her opponent, risking a collision situation in which the windward boat bears the onus of avoiding.

A sudden luffing movement is often used as a bluff. The leading yacht may be fooled into thinking that her opponent is about to tack, and respond only to find her rival has changed her mind and is blithely steaming away on the old course, perhaps into a better wind which she has seen coming her way.

Whatever happens, the leading yacht must make sure that, in her attempts to stay in control, she does not sail beyond the line to the left or right of the course at which point she can sail directly without further tacking straight to the mark.

Four of the eight legs are sailed directly into the wind. Tacking duels are the most exhausting part of America's Cup racing. In a desperate bid to break through from behind the skipper of a trailing yacht may throw as many as 50 tacks in the course of the leg, trying to wrong foot his opponent and force gear or crew failure. Each time his rival is forced to respond he risks splitting the big foresails or snagging the sheets that control them.

As they near the 'top' mark both yachts will have prepared their spinnakers. A quick 'set' is vital for the leading yacht if she is to keep the threat from behind at bay. Downwind, of course, the yacht behind has an advantage as she can get into a position to 'blanket' the yacht ahead. A lead of seven boatlengths at the 'top' mark is the minimum needed to avoid a determined attack from behind.

Upwind

A yacht cannot sail directly into the wind, but a 12 Metre can get closer to it than most. The upwind legs of an America's Cup course (legs 1, 3, 6 and 8) are where most of the gains and losses occur. The shape of the sails and the way they are controlled are as vital as where the helmsman decides to steer and how he attacks his opponent.

In recent years new materials have transformed the look and performance of sails. Kevlar, the distinctive brown-coloured panels, and tough plastic Mylar film give sails strength without stretch, and a shape that can be controlled to give as near perfect aerofoil as possible whatever the wind strength.

Sail shape is controlled in a number of ways – mast bend, mainsheet tension and an almost infinite number of subtle adjustments to control lines. In strong winds the sails are set flatter; fuller in lighter winds. As the wind increases the skipper can call on a range of different headsail sizes and shapes that match the prevailing conditions.

Headsail changes can be made in minutes, the new one is fed up a double tack on the forestay as the old one is wrestled down. Spectators often miss sail changes, so slick is the operation. A flurry of activity as the new sail is brought up from the 'sewer', the bowman precariously perched forward, a shadow passing over the old sail and it's done, bundled below ready for next time.

Downwind

Brightly-coloured spinnakers belie the deadly earnest of the two downwind legs. The skipper who has rounded the 'top' mark first will be praying his lead is enough to keep him beyond the blanketing effect of his opponent the chilling rush of whose bow wave he can hear coming up astern.

Meanwhile his opponent will be urging his crew to renewed efficiency in order to shave vital half seconds off the leading boat's time, trying to edge into the zone where a determined attack could be launched on the yacht ahead.

Good spinnaker shape is the key to downwind speed. Area is not as important as the profile of the sail and its ability to remain stable and not collapse. The brightly coloured panels are not for show. The panels indicate the construction of the sail and how the panels of cloth have been oriented to give maximum stability and strength.

12 Metres seldom sail directly downwind. Invariably the navigator will decide that the yacht will travel faster if she heads to left or right of directly downwind in a series of swoops and gybes (the downwind equivalent of tacking where the sails crash from one side of the yacht to the other in the slickest display of crew work of all).

Spinnakers are flown on legs 2, 4, 5 and 7. The yachts carry a large number of them depending on different wind strengths and conditions. On the two reaching legs (4 and 5) the spinnakers are flatter than the purely downwind spinnakers which tend to be fuller.

Because the yachts very rarely sail directly downwind to the bottom mark, but zigzag (downwind tacking) each change of direction entails precise crew work as the sails are swung over to the other side. Once again the ability of a crew to work smoothly with the minimum delay is the deciding factor.

Many of the tactical decisions downwind are made by careful analysis of electronic instruments. Whether it would pay to head a little more directly for the mark at the expense of speed, or head to left or right of the straight line course and pick up speed at the expense of further distance to be sailed.

Just as in the upwind legs a wind shift can have a dramatic effect on the positions of the protagonists. It's definitely not a time to sit back and allow the wind to blow you down the course. All kinds of pitfalls lie ahead during those agonising, and often painfully slow, 3.25 mile downwind legs.

The leading yacht may sail into a 'hole' while her opponent enjoys free winds astern. Or a fresher wind coming up from behind may enable the trailing yacht to leap ahead those vital boatlengths and blanket her opponent.

It was on just such a downwind leg during the last race of the America's Cup series in 1983 that the Australian yacht broke through from behind to pass clean across the bow of the American yacht, establishing a lead that proved impossible to break.

Australia II's helmsman, John Bertrand, had been trailing the American Dennis Conner up to that point. But sensing more wind on the far side he headed towards it, and because his yacht was able to head downwind as fast or faster than his rival's but at a less acute angle, he was able to slip past; a 21 second lead at the 'bottom' mark was enough to give him the edge on the last leg and Australia's historic victory.

Reaching legs, of which there are two, are often no more than processions. The speeds between two 12 Metres are rarely enough to give either an advantage on this the fastest point of sailing.

The yacht ahead must keep between the next mark and her opponent, warding off any attempted attacks from windward, the side nearest the wind, by luffing her rival into a confusion of flapping sails, before resuming her course to the 'wing' mark – her lead protected and perhaps increased.

If the trailing yacht fails to get past to windward, she may decide to alter course and head across her opponent's stern towards the buoy in order to get inside her rival and 'overlapped' at the buoy – a position which the rules guarantee to uphold free of interference from the outside boat.

Once round, the inside or leading boat is unlikely to be overhauled on the second reaching leg to the 'bottom' or leeward mark. If he can drop his spinnaker swiftly and cleanly he will be able to control the upwind leg from in front. At the mark he may decide to 'stand on' a few boatlengths to see what the boat astern will do and cover accordingly.

Tactically the reaching legs are less interesting, but they more than make up in speed and drama. The loads placed on a 12 Metre's gear, steering system and sails are at their greatest while reaching. This is the time for things to break and for the highest standards in crew work.

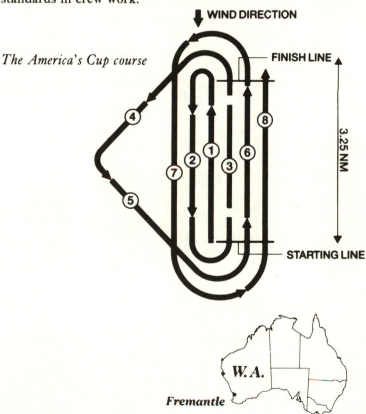

The America's Cup course

WIND DIRECTION

FINISH LINE

3.25 NM

STARTING LINE

W.A.

Fremantle

TABLE OF WINNERS

Year	Challenger	Owner	Club	Defender	Owner	Sco
1851	*America*	John Stevens	New York	*Aurora*		1:0
1870	*Cambria*	James Ashbury	Royal Thames	*Magic*	Franklin Osgood	0:1
1871	*Livonia*	James Ashbury	Royal Harwich	*Columbia/ Sappho*	Osgood Douglas	1:4
1876	*Countess of Dufferin*	Charles Gifford	Royal Canadian	*Madeleine*	John Dickerson	0:2
1881	*Atalanta*	Alexander Cuthbert	Bay of Quinte	*Mischief*	Joseph Busk	0:2
1885	*Genesta*	Sir Richard Sutton	Royal Yacht Squadron	*Puritan*	Forbes Syndicate	0:2
1886	*Galatea*	Lt. William Henn	Royal Northern	*Mayflower*	Charles & Paine	0:2
1887	*Thistle*	Bell Syndicate	Royal Clyde	*Volunteer*	Charles & Paine	0:2
1893	*Valkyrie II*	Earl of Dunraven	Royal Yacht Squadron	*Vigilant*	Iselin Syndicate	0:3
1895	*Valkyrie III*	Earl of Dunraven	Royal Yacht Squadron	*Defender*	Iselin, Morgan & Vanderbilt	0:1
1899	*Shamrock I*	Sir Thomas Lipton	Royal Ulster	*Columbia*	Iselin & Morgan	0:3
1901	*Shamrock II*	Sir Thomas Lipton	Royal Ulster	*Columbia*	J. P. Morgan	0:3
1903	*Shamrock III*	Sir Thomas Lipton	Royal Ulster	*Reliance*	Iselin Syndicate	0:4
1920	*Shamrock IV*	Sir Thomas Lipton	Royal Ulster	*Resolute*	Walters Syndicate	2:3
1930	*Shamrock V*	Sir Thomas Lipton	Royal Ulster	*Enterprise*	Aldrich Syndicate	0:4
1934	*Endeavour*	Sir T. O. M. Sopwith	Royal Yacht Squadron	*Rainbow*	H. Vanderbilt	2:4
1937	*Endeavour II*	Sir T. O. M. Sopwith	Royal Yacht Squadron	*Ranger*	H. Vanderbilt	0:4
1958	*Sceptre*	Hugh Goodson	Royal Yacht Squadron	*Columbia*	Sears Syndicate	0:4
1962	*Gretel*	Sir Frank Packer	Royal Sydney Yacht Squadron	*Weatherly*	Mercer Frese & Walsh	1:4

ar	Challenger	Owner	Club	Defender	Owner	Score
54	*Sovereign*	A. Boydon	Royal Thames	*Constellation*	Gubelman Syndicate	0:4
57	*Dame Pattie*	Emil Christensen	Royal Sydney Yacht Squadron	*Intrepid*	Intrepid Syndicate	0:4
70	*Gretel II*	Sir Frank Packer	Royal Sydney Yacht Squadron	*Intrepid*	Intrepid Syndicate	1:4
74	*Southern Cross*	Alan Bond	Sun City	*Courageous*	Courageous Syndicate	0:4
77	*Australia*	Alan Bond	Royal Perth	*Courageous*	Kings Point Fund	0:4
80	*Australia*	Alan Bond	Royal Perth	*Freedom*	Fort Schuyler	1:4
83	*Australia II*	Alan Bond	Royal Perth	*Liberty*	Fort Schuyler	4:3
87	*Stars & Stripes*	Sail America Foundation	San Diego	*Kookaburra III*	Taskforce '87	4:0

THE 1987 FINALS

Stars & Stripes v *Kookaburra III*

31 January
Race 1. Wind 10–18 knots
Stars & Stripes wins by one minute 41 seconds

1 February
Race 2. Wind 22–23 knots
Stars & Stripes wins by one minute 10 seconds

2 February
Race 3. Wind 12–18 knots
Stars & Stripes wins by one minute 46 seconds

3 February
Lay day called by *Stars & Stripes*

4 February
Race 4. Wind 16–20 knots
Stars & Stripes wins by one minute 59 seconds